# TRIBAL HOUSING ISSUES

# TRIBAL HOUSING ISSUES

*By*

**Dr. Robin D. Tribhuwan**

*M.A., M.Sc., P.G.D.I.M., Ph.D.*

D P H

DISCOVERY PUBLISHING HOUSE

NEW DELHI-110002

First Published-2005

ISBN 81-7141-917-8



*Published by*

**DISCOVERY PUBLISHING HOUSE**
4831/24, Ansari Road, Prahlad Street,
Darya Ganj, New Delhi-110002 (India)
Phone: 23279245 • Fax: 91-11-23253475
E-mail:dphtemp@indiatimes.com

*Printed at:*
Amit Enterprises, Delhi

# PREFACE

The best and most peaceful place in the world is your own home. It is a place of love, hope and satisfaction. When we return home after work, business or school our feet automatically move towards our next. This is true with the birds, animals and insects as well.

Man is a social animal and is regarded higher than animals because he has the ability to speak, converse has higher degree of rationalisation power and possesses culture. Culture is a totality of socially transmitted behaviour. Its a way of life. Enculturation is a process of learning ones own culture, where in an individual learns about the life style, myths, taboos, customs, traditions and norms of his society.

Every society has certain norms customs, traditions and rituals associated with selecting a site for building a house, and a set behaviour associated with its construction. It is a tendency of the owner of the house that he completes the cultural obligations and rituals so as to find peace in the new 'Vastu' or home. The Hindu society has made provision of the science of building a house called "Vastu Shastra".

Tribals too have cultural norms, taboos, traditions, customs and rituals associated with house construction. They value these, as they mean a lot to them. Every social action in the context of house building ritual is hence meaningful to the tribals. Besides, they are used to staying in a particular house pattern in a given ecological environment for ages so as to withstand the same. For example the tribal huts of western Maharashtra in the Konkan region have low roofs because of the sea. The houses of Naga, Lepcha and Madia are built on wooden beams leaving 3 to 5 feet high space above the ground to prevent wild animals from entering the house. Their houses are on mountains and in thick forests where wild animal are found.

It is therefore necessary to keep in view the cultural and ecological aspects associated with tribal housing, their socio-economic background and purchasing power, before planning housing projects for them. This book throws light on these aspects. Facts analysed and interprected in this study will be of immense help to policy makers, administrators, architects, building contractors as well as social science students to plan, implement, monitor and follow-up culturally and ecologically appropriate house designs and settlement patterns for the tribal lot. The book will also be useful to researchers, N.G.O's and development agencies involved in housing projects.

I am grateful to Mrs. Gauri Purandare for doing the sketches of the tribal houses. Lastly I would like to express my gratitude to Mrs. Sandhya Kurde for typing the manuscript.

**Dr. Robin D. Tribhuwan**

M.A., M.Sc, P.G.D.I.M., Ph.D.

# CONTENTS

# CONTENTS

# CHAPTER—1

# TRIBAL HOUSING ISSUES: EMIC AND ETIC PERSPECTIVES

## 1.1 Profile of Tribal Settlements

Nearly 69 millions of India's population is tribal, most of who live in accessible areas, i.e. on the hills and mountains, in the forests and valleys. Every tribe has developed culture specific ways and means to design their settlements and housing patterns. Depending on the natural resources such as timber, sticks, bamboos, leaves etc. available within the ecosystem, the tribes have evolved design of their settlements and houses. They also perform several rituals before, during and after constructing the house. Some tribes perform rituals to protect their village boundaries. The Kolams of Yavatmal district in Maharashtra perform a ritual called "gaon bandhani", wherein they appease the deity of the village boundary to protect the village.

A tribal settlement is composed of small number of huts popularly known as a hamlet. The number of huts in a hamlet vary from 10 to 200. In Maharashtra tribal hamlets are known as "Wadis" or "Padas". A "Padas" or "Wadi" comprises of a single tribe or two or more tribes. Most tribal padas usually comprise of one major tribe. Some tribal hamlets are part of a major caste village.

Tribal hamlets on the plains i.e. closer to caste villages are in a group, while those ones in the valleys, on the mountains etc., in inaccessible areas tend to have a scattered nature. The Bhil Padas of Satpuda mountain range are typically scattered type of hamlets.

In his book captioned, "The Warlis", Save K.J. (1945: 18) states that some of the note worthy points about Warli hamlets. These are, Warli hamlets are not segregated locality as a "Mahar wada" or a "Katwada", i.e. the settlements of the then untouchable caste groups. Secondly, he states that a Warli hamlet is not styled Warli wada, though Warlis prefer to live in a locality seperate from that of the higher classes, they admit members of other tribes like Dublas, Dhodias or Koknas in their midst.

Layout of tribal hamlet varies from tribe to tribe. The Katkaris of Maharashtra prefer to build houses in a line opposite to each others houses, so as to create a lane in the centre. The Thakars build their houses close to each other, so as to form a clustered hamlet. On the other hand Bhils of Satpuda who live on the mountains and hills and in the valleys, live in scattered houses. Tribal settlement phenomena itself is very interesting. Some of the characteristics of tribal settlement in India are as follows:

*(i)* Every tribal hamlet has a traditional boundary.

*(ii)* The village deity is mostly within/or on the village boundary. In Maharashtra tribal village deities are known as goan dev or devi.

*(iii)* The location of tribal village deities in India is either east, west or north, but never south.

*(iv)* Burial or cremation grounds are towards the south.

*(v)* Defecation grounds for males and females are seperate.

## 1.2 Tribal Housing Patterns.

A reader of this book can very well understand a tribal house pattern by reading the description of a ' Thakar ' house. In his book captioned, " The Thakars of Syhadri ", Chaphekar L.N. (1961: 8 - 11) has described the Thakar house as follows:

A small Thakar house has only one entrance and one of overage size two. One of the entrance opens into the cattleshed. The house door faces either east, north or west. The house is usually squarish in shape and is on an area of 200 to 800 sq.feet. The traditional house has a thatched roof and walls made up of Karvi sticks. These sticks are smeared with cowdung.

Stones are used for the plinth, if any. Over it stands the wooden frame work walled by wattle and daub. Usually one or two families live in a hut. Majority of Thakars live in nuclear families. During rainy season a Thakar family grows vegetables in the Kitchen garden. The house has a compound made up of bamboos or wooden sticks with a small gate during rainy season. Given below are sketches showing tribal houses.

## 1.3 Status of Tribal Housing in Maharashtra: An etic view

The Tribal Research and Training Institute conducted a Bench Mark Survey in 2001 in the entire T.S.P. area of Maharashtra on various development indicators. Given below are three tables which reveal an etic (outsider's) view about the houses of tribals in Maharashtra.

**Table No. 1.1: Households classified according to ownership of houses**

| Sr.No. | Type of ownership | No. of household | % with total |
|---|---|---|---|
| 1. | Own House | 586882 | 92.48 |
| 2. | Indira Awas | 31100 | 4.90 |
| 3. | Housing Society | 1585 | 0.25 |
| 4. | Rented | 10970 | 1.73 |
| 5. | Others | 4043 | 0.64 |
| | **Total** | **634580** | **100.00** |

*Source:* B.M.S. Household Report No. 4

From the table 1.1 it is clear that nearly 92.48 % of the tribals in Maharashtra have their own house, where as only 4.90 % benifitted from the Indira Awas Housing Scheme. There is therefore an urgent need to work out a culturally acceptable and ecologically appropriate housing plan for the tribals. Despite of 55 years of independence, tribals of Maharashtra still live in huts. Table no. 1.2 reveals that 74.67 % of Tribals in T.S.P. area of Maharashtra still live in Kucha house, i.e. without brick walls. Sketches of houses of different tribes are shown by the author so that a reader gets an idea of how tribal houses are.

Diagram No.1 (THAKAR)

Sketch of a Thakar hut, from the State of Maharashtra, India

Diagram No. 2

Inner sketch of a Thakar House, from the State of Maharashtra, India

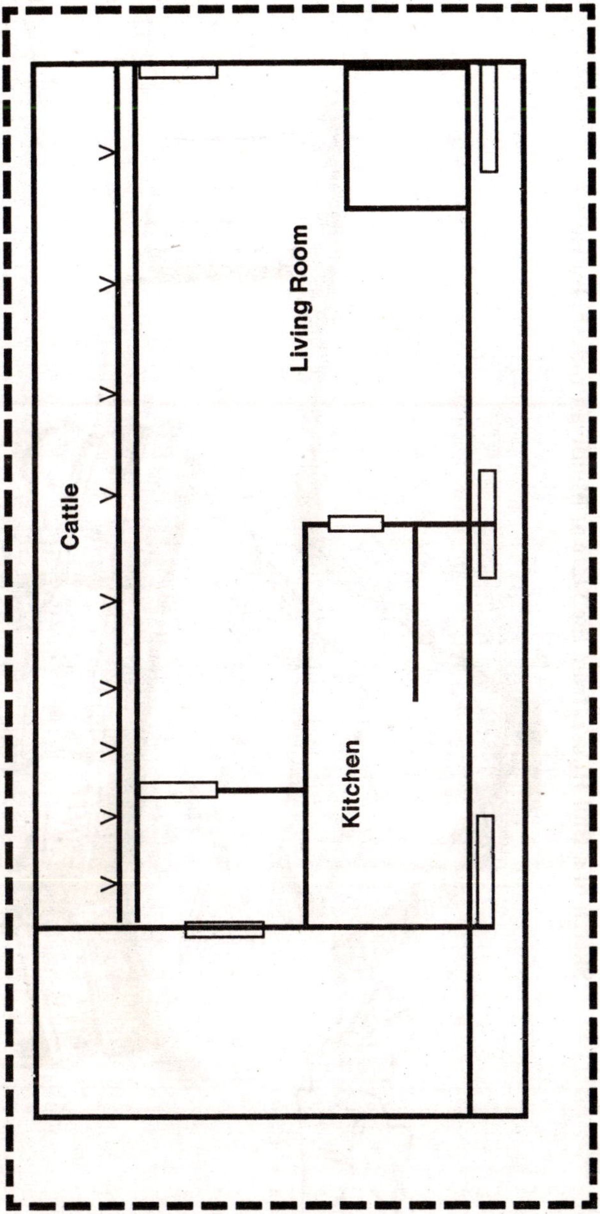

Diagram No. 3 (BHIL)

Sketch of a Bhil House, from the State of Madhya Pradesh, India

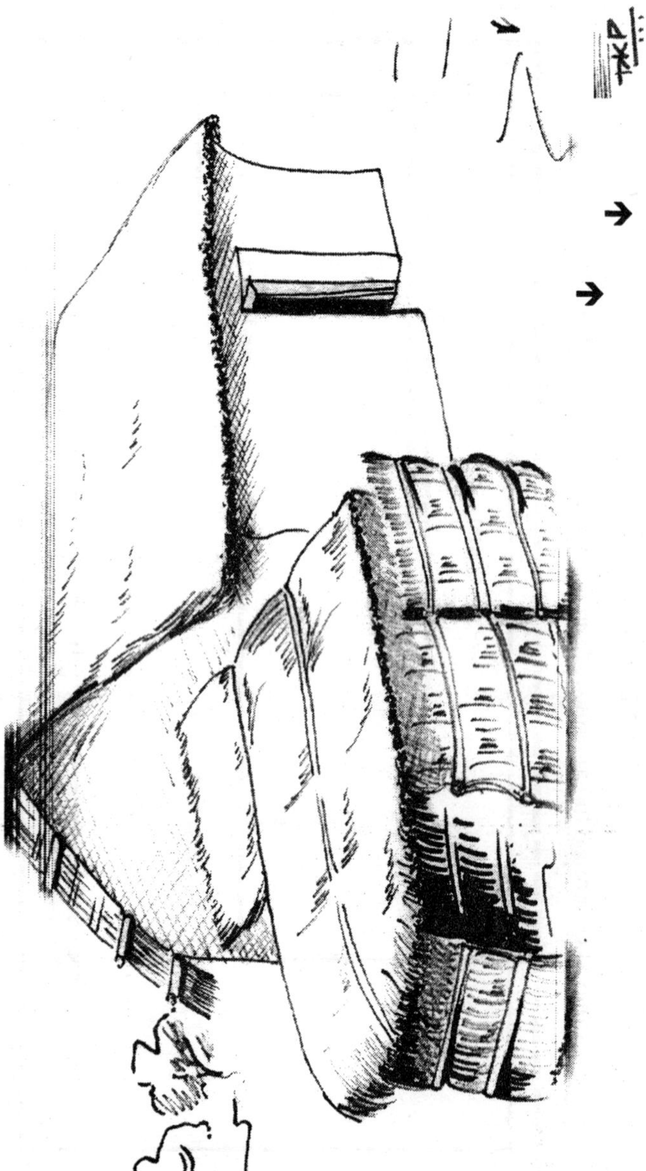

Diagram No. 4 (BIRHOR)

Sketch of a Birhor house, from the State of Bihar, in India

Diagram No. 5 (NAGA)

Sketch of Naga House, from Nagaland, in India

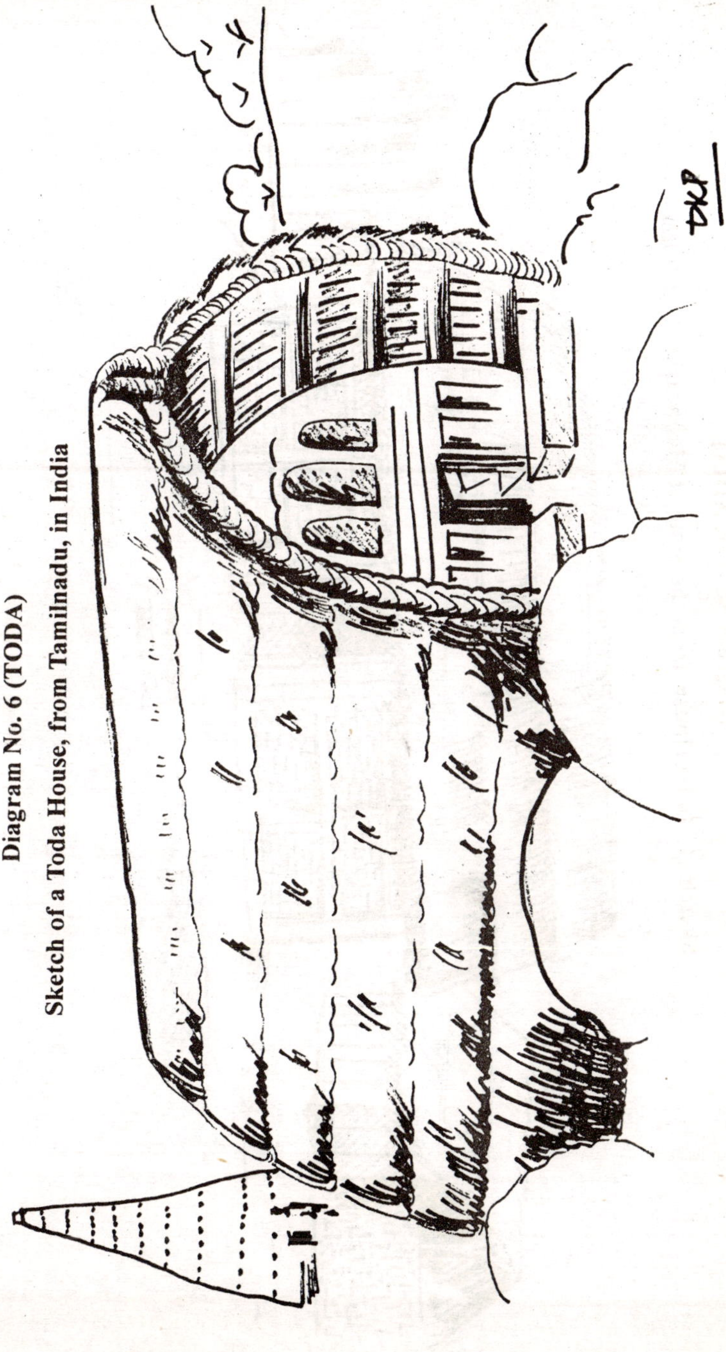

Diagram No. 6 (TODA)

Sketch of a Toda House, from Tamilnadu, in India

Diagram No. 7 (MADIA)

Sketch of Madia House, from the State of Maharashtra, in India

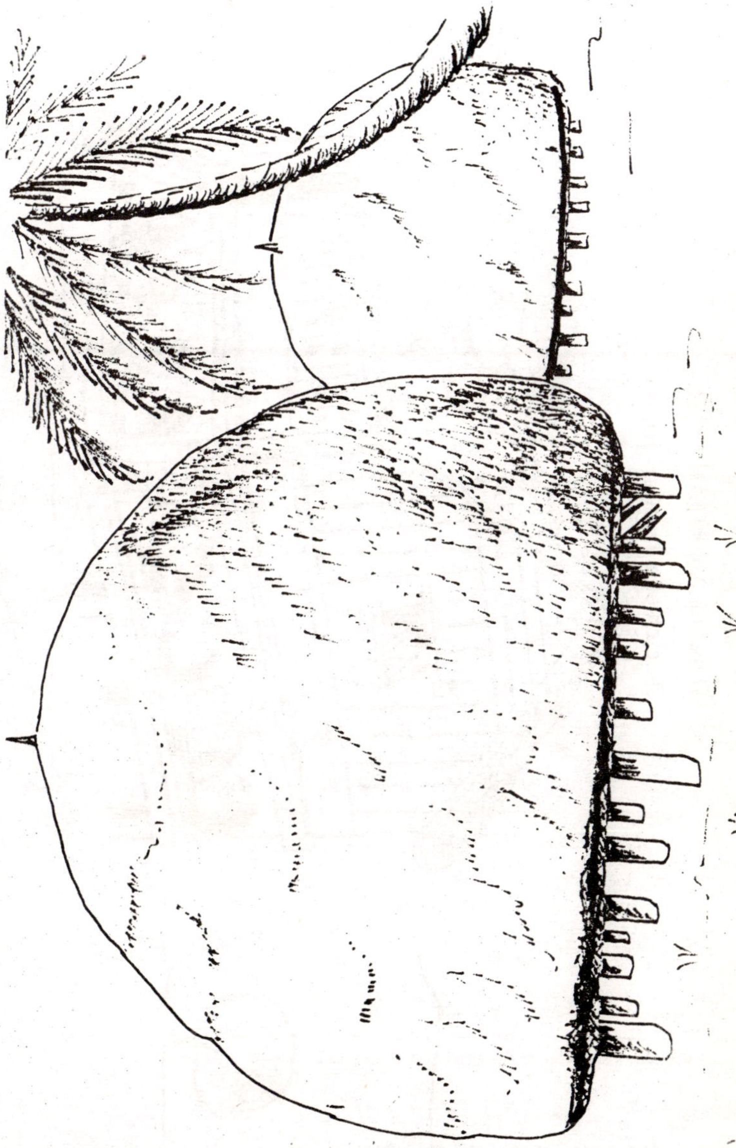

Diagram No. 8 (NICOBARESS)

Sketch of a Nicobari House, from Car Nicobar, India

Diagram No. 9 (JAUNSARI)

Sketch of a Jaunsari House

Diagram No. 10 (ORAON)

Sketch of a Oraon House

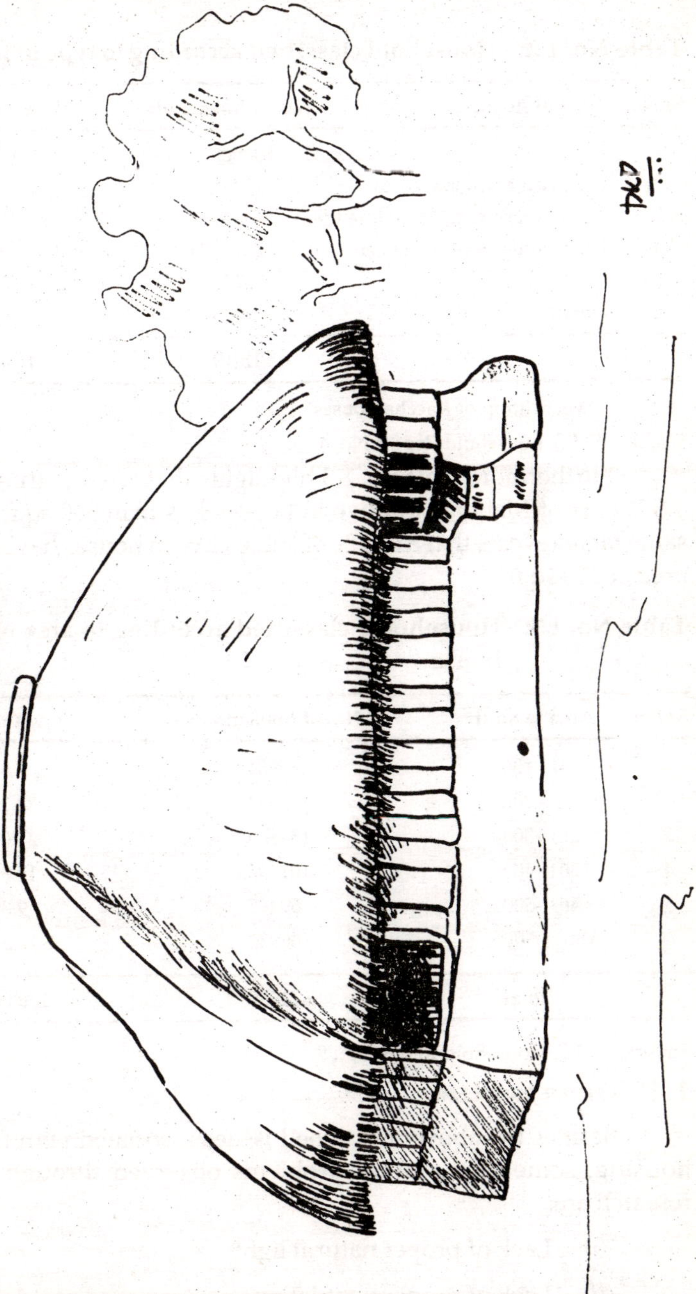

**Table No. 1.2: Household classified according to type of house**

| Sr.No. | Type of house | No. of households | % with total |
|---|---|---|---|
| 1. | Hut* | 100506 | 15.84 |
| 2. | Hut with Manglore tiles* | 373298 | 58.83 |
| 3. | Pacca house with Manglore tiles | 133449 | 21.03 |
| 4. | Pacca house with tin sheets | 20589 | 3.24 |
| 5. | R.C.C. | 2995 | 0.47 |
| 6. | Others | 3743 | 0.59 |
| | **Total** | **634580** | **100.00** |

Classification of Kaccha houses*

*Source:* B.M.S. household Report No. 4

Furthermore table no. 1.3 highlights that 82.68 % tribals in T.S.P. area of Maharashtra live in houses less than 500 sq.ft. The same table reveals that 57.31 % of tribals live in houses having an area of 300 sq.ft.

**Table No. 1.3: Households classified according to area of the house**

| Sr.No. | Area in sq.ft. | No. of households | % with total |
|---|---|---|---|
| 1. | 0 - 100 | 49904 | 7.86 |
| 2. | 101 - 200 | 179954 | 28.36 |
| 3. | 201 -300 | 133805 | 21.09 |
| 4. | 301 -400 | 101490 | 15.99 |
| 5. | 401 -500 | 59495 | 9.38 |
| 6. | Above 500 | 109932 | 17.32 |
| | **Total** | **634580** | **100.00** |

Source: B.M.S. Household Report No. 5

## 1.4 Other Problems

Besides the above mentioned issues associated with tribal housing, some of the other problems observed through this research are:

*(i)* Lack of proper natural light.

*(ii)* Lack of proper ventilation.

*(iii)* Dampness on the floor.

*(iv)* Smoky houses due to lack of proper ventilation and presence of smokeless chulas.

*(v)* Lack of adequately planned houses.

*(vi)* Lack of drainage system.

*(vii)* Lack of toilets and bathrooms.

*(viii)* Lack of awareness among tribals regarding housing schemes.

*(ix)* Lack of education material in both audio, visual and written forms for the tribals.

*(x)* Lack of interdisciplinary and/or anthropological studies before planning housing projects.

## 1.5 STATEMENT OF THE PROBLEM.

The international academic community debates over two issues related to tribals. These are:

*(i)* Should tribals/indigenous/native people live where they are in their original state ?

or

*(ii)* Should the welfare democratic state of which they are a part disturb them to develop them ?

If we leave them to themselves, they may maintain their culture and heritage, but will remain poor, hungry, illiterate and socially backward. If we develop them, they will change, to loose their culture and heritage. Should they enjoy the benefits of the Welfare State like the non-tribals is a matter that concerns human rights and communal harmony ?

As an Anthropologist and Development expert, I am of the opinion that tribals have the right to develop, progress and change for better. However, it depends both on the tribals as well the Welfare State to work hand in hand to preserve tribal heritage and culture. This can be done by establishing museums, by preserving traditional dance forms, music, dramas, songs etc.

Secondly tribals must get to live in brickmade, cement concrete houses at least with a tiled roof if not a concrete roof. Similarly efforts should be made to keep tribal traditions so as to preserve their culture.

## 1.6 Aim of the Book

This book aims to present tribal housing issues in India, with reference to Maharashtra keeping in view following aims.

*(a)* To study the problems associated with tribal housing from an etic perspective.

*(b)* To unravel the symbolism that tribal associate to construction, designs and layout of their houses.

*(c)* To impress upon the policy makers, administrators, community organisers, educators and other development agents, the need to conduct an interdisciplinary study and anthropological documentation associated with tribal housing, before planning these projects for them.

*(d)* To suggest recommendations to plan, implement, monitor and follow-up culturally acceptable and ecologically appropriate housing projects for the tribals.

## 1.7 Significance of the Book

The Theoretical purpose of the study will be to show how the set of normative actions (symbols & meanings) performed during the process of planning & constructing a tribal house, works out of a basic central meaning system and that it will be possible for the anthropologists to engird the organising structure of the complex symbols & meanings of a tribal culture by restricting themselves to a single area of social life (in this context tribal housing patterns).

In doing so the study intends to demonstrate that the traditional house designs, patterns, layout & rituals associated with it are meaningful to the members of the tribe concerned. That, these actions need to be respected and valued before making any housing project plans for the tribals.

At the more practical level data on symbolism of tribal housing patterns & designs will be immense use to policy makers, administrators & those involved in carrying out housing schemes and programs for the tribals.

The book also provides a methodology of understanding traditional tribal housing patterns. It suggests recommendations to policy makers, regarding how to go about planning tribal housing projects.

*****

# CHAPTER—2

# RESEARCH METHODOLOGY

## 2.1 Setting of the Study

The study is an outcome of research on tribal housing patterns of major tribes in Maharashtra, Madhya Pradesh, Rajasthan and Gujarat. The author has been visiting tribal villages since 1985 for research and development work through out India. During the course of time special attention was given to understand tribal housing issues.

## 2.2 The People

Although the analysis and interpretation reflects data and observation of several tribal housing patterns. The major tribes focussed in the study were Bhils, Madia, Koknas, Katkaris or Kathodis, Thakars, Nagas, Gonds, Warlis etc.

## 2.3 Method of Data Collection

Informal in-depth interviews and case studies were used to document the primary data. Observation method was used to cross-check data collected through interviews and case studies. The program of Indira Awas Housing Yojana was evaluated in some villages to explore the gaps. Primary data is supported with photographs and sketches.

## 2.4 Analysis

Since the data is qualitative it was analysed manually. An analysis of how the tribals associated the cultural symbols and meanings with house construction to other domains of social life was done.

## 2.5 Chapter Scheme

The primary and secondary data reported, analysed and incorporated in this book is presented in five chapters namely;

1. **Chapter One:** "Tribal Housing Issues: Emic and Etic perspectives", as the name suggests provides an account of traditional housing patterns and the tribal perceptions associated with design creations and rituals of construction from their perspective. An effort has been made to highlight how an outsider looks at housing projects from his perspective.
2. **Chapter Two:** "Research Methodology". The second chapter presents the methodology used by the researcher in gathering, analyzing and interpreting primary and secondary data.
3. **Chapter Three:** "Traditional Tribal Housing Layout: A symbolic analysis", is presented in the form of case studies to explore the symbols and meanings tribal associated with house construction and designs of the same.
4. **Chapter Four:** "Status of Tribal housing scheme: An overview", provides an analysis of status, condition and the gaps the exist in the tribal housing program planning, implementation, monitoring and follow-up.
5. **Chapter Five:** Summary, conclusion and recommendations. In the last chapter an attempt has been made to place on record conclusions of the study and few recommendations to provide to good housing to the tribals as well as maintain their cultural heritage.

*****

# CHAPTER—3

# TRADITIONAL TRIBAL HOUSING LAYOUT: A SYMBOLIC ANALYSIS

## 3.1 Concept of Symbolism

Symbolization is an universal human process. It is the most important human trait man can create symbols. Through symbols ideas and meanings are represented. Richard Cavendish (1985: 258-75) states that a symbol by definition is not what it represents. It stands for suggests and reveals a mind a reality other than itself. He further states that the function of symbols is to act as a " rallying point for meaning ". through it the mind connects several meanings.

Symbols have been analyzed by logicians, metaphysicians, linguists, psychologists, theologicians, historians and folklorists, but the anthropological approach is expected to be comparative, observationist, functionalists and relative neutralist. It links the occurrence in a society and interpretation of symbols to social structure and social events in specific condition.

Anthropologists observe symbols, study them so as to understand their meanings in the larger cultural contexts from an insider's perspective. Emphasis is laid on exploring how people derive meanings out of symbols ? How they co-relate them and how these symbols are finally organized into a system. This inturn helps an Anthropologist to understand social life as a meaningful system. The above theorotical discussion certainly proves that every social action in an actual context is meaningrul and that is why it performed by the participant actors in the ritual setting.

Symbolism associated with all the rituals of house lay out and construction is meaningful too. In this chapter an attempt has been made to impress upon an administrator, policy maker or a development agency involved in planning and implementing tribal housing projects, how important it is to understand the symbolism in tribal housing. Secondly, before planning any housing construction scheme for tribals how important it is to respect their cultural values associated with house building. Unless & until we understand what their traditional beliefs and practices regarding house design, layout and construction are, it is quite possible that the programs will create resistence from the tribals or maybe a failure even.

To make the above thecretical view more practical and clear an examples of he Thakar and Warli house symbolism is given below.

## 3.2 Tribal Housing layout and cosmos

### *(a) Aada: The God of Rains*

In his book Captioned Medical World of Tribals (Tribhuwan Robin 1998) has stated how Thakars associate the layout and design of their traditional house with the cosmos. According to the Thakars their houses which are sqvarish in shape have four directions namely North, South, East & West. The roof symbolizes the sky. An horizontal wooden piece of wood called "Aada " made up of " Jamun tree ' (Eugenia jambolina) on which the attached roof rests is a symbol of " Rain God ". During construction of the house, the Thakars offer a coconut so as to appeare the God of rains. They pray to the God of rains (Aada) to prevent their roof from leaking. They tie a coconut in the cloth and tie it around the " Aada ".

### *(b) Mothur med: Sun God*

Towards th south east is the " mothur med " (Teak wooden pillar), it is a symbol of " Sun " (Suryadev). This is the first pillar errected by five Thakar males, who insert the pillar in the hole. Thakars believe that the act of insertion of "mothur med" is symbolic of he sexual union of sun with earth.. this results into a family.

### *(c) Chul: Holi Goddess*

The Chul or "hearth" or fire place which is situated towards the south east is a symbol of "Holi" - sister of the sun. Thakars believe that because of "Holi" - fire, they can cook food and hence fire to them is a cosmic force like the sun, rain, earth etc. which helps them to survive, is a significant cosmic force. Well, these and several other examples can be cited to show how tribals link house designs and layout with cosmos.

## 3.3 Anti-clock placement of pillars

Yet another interesting aspect observed by Dr. Tribhuwan Robin (1998) was after the "mothur med" is fixed the thakars then fix other three pillars in an anticlock fashion. They believe all elements and forces in the cosmos move in an anticlock manner. For example clouds according to Thakars move in an anticlock fashion. The blood in the body moves in an anticlock manner. Therefore all rituals in the Thakar community, which involves circular movement is anticlock movement. Most tribes have the anticlock movement ritual in their respective culture, as it is considered to be auspicious. Where as in the Hindu culture clock wise movement is considered to be auspicious. For example the retual of "sapta pada", i.e. seven steps around the fire during the wedding is done in a clockwise fashion.

The moral of the above fact is that, the tribals even take into consideration small aspects such as anticlock placement and fixing of pillar, during construction of their houses. These rituals and actions to them are meaningful and that is why they enact them during construction of their houses.

## 3.4 Role of a shaman

A shaman (Bhagat), who is a diviner and interpretor of supernatural phenomena presides over several village rituals of the Thakars. He plays as important role in site selection. He performs rituals to identify any obstacle, barrier, any evil eliment on the ground where the house has to be built. After performing the ritual of site selection, in case of any evil element or force on the site, he performs the ritual of purification.

## 3.5 Rituals of Purification

The shamans perform several rituals of purification of land on which the house has to be built. Some of them are as follows:

### *(i) Sprinkling of Holy Water*

Water is considered to be the brother of sun by the Thakars. It is a symbol of purification and is believed to cleanse evil.

### *(ii) Sacrifice of a Poultru Fowl*

A black chicken is sacrificed if a shaman identifies any evil spirit or force on the land. The spirit is offered a sacrifice so that he or she does not create any hinderance or causes problems to the occupant of the land.

### *(iii) Nailing the Evil Spirits*

Some times a shaman takes a old leather slipper and nailing it into the ground. The Thakars believe that the shaman nails the spirit so that he does not disturb the occupant. It is quite possible that these kind of rituals may vary from one tiribe to another, not only in India, but throughout the world.

## 3.6 Direction Symbolism

Direction play a signigicant role in tribal house layout and disigns. For example no tribal house door faces the house. they believe here in Maharashtra that the south is an evil direction called "Rakshas Disha" - the direction wherein demons dwell. Hence south is an evil direction. The tribal burial grounds are situated towards south. When a dead body is burried the posture of the body is such that its head points towards the south.

Thus, while sleeping, relaxing, resting, having sex, or even while delivering a child, tribals prefer as a cultural rule to point their heads towards North, East or West, but not the "Rakshas Disha" - the evil south. Among the Hindu "Vastu Shashtra" too south is considered to be evil.

## 3.7 House design and health

Given below is an illness episode cited from Dr. Robin Tribhuwan's book, namely, "Medical World of Tribals (1998: 88-97)", to illustrate the co-relation of tribal house design with their health.

# ILLNESS EPISODE

### Aim

1. To highlight how illness experience crosscuts meanings of human body as a social, religious and cosmological symbol.
2. To study the various conceptions of a Thakar involved in house building.
3. To study the material culture.
4. To explore the concept of evil spirits.
5. To explore the symbolic aspects related to childbirth.

### Background

Mrs. Dharma Pardhi, 28 years, married female. Both she and her husband Mr. Pardhi were working for a voluntary organization viz. Academy of Development Science (A.D.S.) . Their native settlement Borwadi is 1 km. away from A.D.S. Mr. Pardhi worked in a dairy and Mrs. Pardhi worked in the cafeteria. Their working hours required both of them to be most of the time at A.D.S. Hence they were given a house near the dairy on the campus itself.

The A.D.S. has built good concrete house for its employees. This house (given to Mr & Mrs Pardhi) did not meet the Thakars concept of house building. The Pardhi family stayed on the A.D.S. campus for seven years. During this period they changed their home twice for a number of reasons. Some of the major reasons are highlighted in this episode.

### Course of Events

During this period of seven years Mrs. Pardhi faced a lot of trouble and was sick on several occasions.

### Illness and Trouble in the New House

During the first year, in the new house on the A.D.S. campus, Mr & Mrs Pardhi often fell sick. Either or both of them would fall sick every month. The following year two of their pet cats died and their son suffered from chicken pox in the third year.

### Request for a new house

After suffering from a spate of calamities spread over a period of three years, the Pardhi decided to request the authorities for a change of house. They believed that this house was unlucky for them.

### Setting of the new house

The second house allotted to them was also near the dairy. It had many clutural drawbacks according to the Thakars. To enlist them, the door of the house faced south. The southern direction is believed to be evil, the hearth (chulah) was in the north-eastern direction, there was no 'Mothur-med' (the first pillar which symbolizes the Sun God), there was no 'Aada' (a horizontal jamun wooden pole fixed below the roof). This 'Aada' symbolizes the sky. There was no central place for grinding rice. Overlooking these cultural drawbacks Mr. & Mrs. Pardhi lived in the second house for a period of four years.

### Disaster in the second house

Mr. and Mrs. Pardhi found that after shifting to the second house their luck and fortune had taken a turn for the worse. Trouble, sickness, misery were their constant companions in the second house. The calamities which came upon them can be enumerated as follows:

1. Constant prevalence of sickness in the family for seven years.
2. Two cats died in the first house.
3. One calf died in the second house.
4. Both Mrs Pardhi and her son suffered from chicken pox.
5. The construction of the house did not meet the Thakar's cultural building style.
6. Mrs Pardhi lost her job as the cafe incharge in the A.D.S. cafeteria.

7. The 'Baya' -a band of Goddesses symbolizing the planets would visit Mrs Pardhi every Tuesday and Thursday and would go into a trance.
8. Their village God 'Bhairi' - considered to be the brother of the Sun God (life giver) appeared to Mrs Pardhi in her dreams and would tell her to change her house from A.D.S. campus to Borwadi (Their native village).

## On Consulting A Bhagatin (Female Shaman)

'Mrs Pardhi, did you discuss your problems with anyone?' Pat, came the reply 'Yes, of course I consulted a Bhagatin of Kotimba village.'

The Bhagatin was given Rs. 1.25 to diagnose the origin and cause of the troubles and illnesses which fell on the Pardhi family.

The Bhagatin lit an incense stick, offered a coconut to the 'Baya' - the planetary Goddesses. She then went into a trance during which she moved in a clockwise direction and started reciting the mantras. She interpreted that Mrs Pardhi's trouble and sickness was because of the warth of the 'Baya'. The 'Baya' were annoyed with the Pardhi's because they stayed in the A.D.S. houses which were not built according to the culturally recognized norms of the Thakar society. Mrs Pardhi was asked to shift back to Borwadi and was given a necklace (Gala patta) made of aluminum which symbolizes that Mrs Pardhi was a devotee of the 'Baya'. She was also instructed to offer a coconut to the Baya after shifting to her native sttlement in Borwadi.

## From A.D.S. to Borwadi

When Mrs Pardhi heard the divine instructions from the Bhagatin and the call of the Baya, she discussed the matter with her husband and her in-laws. They also agreed and so Mr & Mrs Pardhi shifted out of the A.D.S.premises. They settled in a culturally designed house and are living here since the past two years. When asked about any troubles, they replied 'We are perfectly happy and free from all troubles.'

## Analysis

Mr. & Mrs. Pardhi firmly bellieved that a Thakar house brought good luck and house built by the A.D.S. brought ill-luck to them. They gave information about the cultural significance of building a house (in a particular way) which is nothing but a reflection of cosmos. The cosmos in turn is reflection of the human body and therefore there is a very close relationship between the human body and the cosmic objects that exist in the universe.

## Layout and Construction of a Thakar house

When a Thakar builds his house, he abides by the cultural rules and regulations regarding the building of a house. Thus, the various rituals and ceremonies, concerned with every step of house building are religiously followed. Some of the rituals are concerned with finding a suitable place for the house, digging the earth and placing the first pillar (Mothur-med) which symbolizes the sun, worshipping the pillar, fixing in the anticlockwise direction the remaining three pillars and so on. These rituals are symbolic and meaningful to the Thakars.

### 1. The Mothur Med (The support of the house)

A wooden pillar of teak is known as mothur med. The head of the house digs a hole five feet in depth and puts some gulal (red powder) and rice grains in the hole. Then, five men including the head of the family erect the pillar firmly into the hole.

The pillar is symbolic of the sun, head of the Universe and the hole symbolizes the mother Earth. The fixing of the mothur med into the hole is symbolic of the sexual relationship between the sun and the earth (male and female cosmic forces). A coconut is offered which symbolizes the spermatic flow of the sun, into the earth. The rice placed in the hole symbolizes the fertility of the family. The participation of males symbolizes their dominance and their sexual role. Thus fixing of the mothur med is meaningful and symbolic of establishing a family.

Thus the mothur med is very significant in building a house as it is symbolic of the Sun (the life giver and supporter of humanity). The next phase is that of worshipping the mothur med.

The head of the family ties a black cloth to the pole. In the cloth are various things viz, Biba (Semicarpus anacardium), Halad (Aurcuma Domestica), Supari (Areca catechu) and gulal (a red powder). These objects are ritualistically tied to prevent and ward off the external evil effect on the house. The mothur med is fixed towards the south-east.

### The Fixing of Other Three Poles

After the mothur med is fixed the other three poles are fixed in an anticlockwise manner. This is done because the Thakars believe that the sum moves in an anticlockwise direction from the east to the west round the earth. They also believe that the wind, clouds and other cosmic movement is also in the anticlock direction.

## 2. The Hearth (Chulah—Goddess of Fire)

Towards the south-east next to the mothur med is the hearth. It faces the west. This is so done, so that the woman while cooking should face the east - the direction of life because the sun rises there. The fire of the chul symbolizes 'Holi' a goddess of 'Agni' (fire) who. the Thakars believe is the sister of the sun. The chul is thus holy and a symbol of purity, as it contains fire which helps to purify and cook raw food.

The ash (Surya Rakhad)in the chul is considered holy and symbolizes the body of the sun. All medical practitioners including Bhagats and Bhagatins (male and female Shaman), Vaidu (Herbalist). had vaidu (Bone stter), Midwife (Suine).the Mantrik (Snake and Scorpion sting specialists) and the potdhari (help mate of the midwife) use the holy ash for performing healing rites.

### The Purification of the Hearth

Although the hearth is believed to be the symbol of purity, it is cleansed and purified ritually on many occasions. One such occasion is on the solar eclipse. On this day the hearth or the chul is not used at all, which means that Thakars do not cook on this day. It is believed that the Sun (Life giver) is covered with darkness (evil) and hence all the food items and water lose their power and strength and become evil. The evil effect of darkness pollutes the almighty Sun and makes it impure and blocks the light giving holy rays of the Sun. After the eclipse, all vegetables, grains and other food items are washed ritually with water (the purifier and brother of Sun).

The Thakars especially the pregnant women fast on solar eclipse. After the eclipse is over, the hearth is plastered with cowdung and water. This act symbolizes the purification and cleansing of the evil effect of darkness on the hearth. The ash from the hearth symbolizes the remains of the Sun and the hearth or chul is symbolic of the Goddess of Agni (Holi). These two, symbolize the company of the divine forces with the Thakars. Some other occasions on which the hearth is purified are -

1. During the 'Pitra Amosha' (a festival of ancestral spirits). the Thakars believe that their ancestral spirits come and visit them.
2. On the fifth day after the delivery to welcome the 'Satvai'—the mother earth. It is believed that she comes in the form of a bird or an animal to write the 'life span' of the new born by making a mark on the child's forehead.
3. The hearth is plastered when a menstruating woman completes her menses. Before she cooks she must bathe, wash her clothes and then purify the hearth by plastering it.

Cowdung thus symbolize an object which holds the power to ward effect, purify and also neutralize the evil effect. When a person is affected which or by the evil eye, cowdung is ritually used to absorb the evil effect.

Thus, presence of the hearth and its position in the south-east is very meaningful to the Thakars.

## 3. The Kitchen, Dining Cum Delivery Room

The kitchen where the hearth is placed is used for cooking and dining. It also doubles up as a place for delivery. The pregnant women lies down facing the west about five feet away from the hearth. The delivery posture is never North-South as south is the direction of death, while north, east and west are directions of life.

### 4. Sleeping place

The central place in the house is used for sleeping by the Thakars. It is in this area that the rice is ground and pounded. In the center of the room there is a hole known as 'Ukhali'. 'Ukhali' is made of stone and is used for pounding rice and to separate the husk. Pounding is always done by the woman.

### 5. Cattle Shed

Cattle are looked upon with great affection and considered to be children by the Thakars. Hence they are tied in the house itself. this is so because the livelihood of the Thakars depend on the cattle.

### 6. The Rakshas Disha (The evil south)

The south (direction) is believed to be the dwelling place of evil spirits, giants and bad forces. It is therefore termed as "Rakshas Disha". Even the air and wind which blow from the south are believed to bring illness. trouble and death. As the south, symbolizes the direction of death, the Thakars bury their dead with the head pointing to the south.

Even while sleeping or resting, the Thakars never sleeps with the head pointing south. He rests, pointing either North, East or West. It is believed that magicians, witches, sorcers get their evil powers from the south. All evil acts are performed facing south.

### 7. The East "Ungvat Baju"

Of all the directions, the east is believed to be most important of all. The main significance attached to the east is that the Sun (life-giver) comes up (rises) from here and hence all good activities, rituals and ceremonies are performed facing the east. Some of the rituals are given below.

1. Diagnosis of illness (performing diagnostic rites).
2. Collection, preparation and administration of medicine is done facing the east.
3. All village GODS face the east.
4. Drummers performing Dhambdi (dance performed by elders) and Gauri dance (dance performed by youngsters) facing the east.

5. Rituals connected with offering food, sacrifice and coconut are performed facing the east.
6. All actions, rituals and ceremonies which aim to bring good fortune to the Thakar society are performed facing the east.
7. The air/wind which symbolizes life is believed to flow anticlockwise from east to west.

East is believed to have a good effect on Thakar life and thus is symbolic of "life" and "good omen" heaven (swarg) is believed to be situated in the east.

## 8. The Mavalat Disha (the West)

The west direction is the direction of "Goddess Satvai" (The Goddess of fortune, life span and fertility). Goddess satvai is none other than Mother Earth. She faces the sun in the west, while it is in the east. The wind blowing from the west carries with it the spirits of "Baya" - the nine planets (Sisters of mother earth). On the fifth day after the delivery the satvai comes from the west to visit the child and to write its life span on the forehead.

## 9. The Dev Disha (The Holy North)

The Thakars believe that the Northern side of the earth is slightly tilted. There are nine lakh steps in this direction which take a person to residence of the Gods.

## 10. The Entrance

The Thakar is guided by the cultural norms and he is allowed to let the entrance of his house face either in the North, East or West direction but never in the Southern direcion.

If the entrance faces the south it is an open invitation to sickness, sorrow, trouble and even death. To the door post are tied five chillies and a lime. The lime is believed to absorb the evil effect while chillies which symbolize hotness (fire) are believed to ward off the effect of the evil eye.

## 11. The Burial Place of the Umbilical Chord

The umbilical chord is buried outside the wall which is in the west. On the inside of the wall is the bathing place of the mother and the new born. The bath water flows out on the umbilical chord buried outside and decays it, thus the chord disappears and is prevented from becoming an object of sorcery and witchcraft.

The ritual of burying the umbilical chord is interesting as it reflects the symbolic and meaningful elements associated with the Thakar's conceptions of sex, fertility, delivery, womanhood, black magic etc. The suine (midwife) takes a palas leaf (Butea monosperma) on which she places the umbilical chord (Nal), the placental waste (Var), rice (chaul), coin (paisa). This leaf is placed in such a way that the apex of the leaf points towards the east and the leaf base towards the west.

**Diagram IV: 1. Showing Umbilical Chord Burial Ritual**

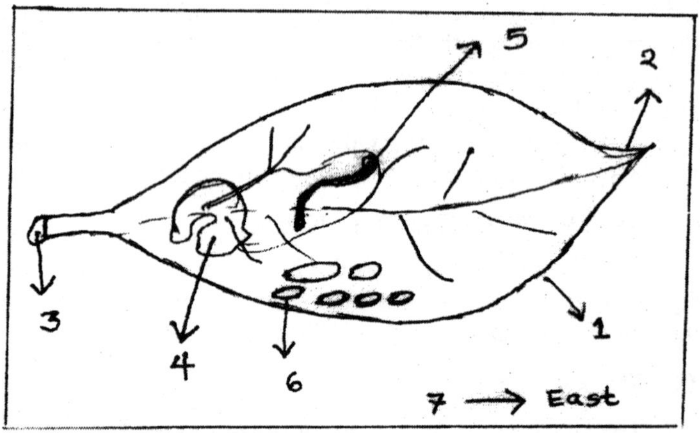


**Meanings**

1. The leaf is symbolic of a fertile woman.
2. The apex symbolizes her head.
3. The base of the petiole symbolizes her vaginal opening.
4. The var symbolizes the womb.
5. The nal symbolizes the child.
6. The rice on the leaf is symbolic of continued fertility.

7. The east west position of the leaf symbolilzes the sexual and delivery posture of woman.

8. The dorsal surface of the leaf is symbolic of the woman's desire for children and sex. Chaphekar (1961) reports that if the midwife turns the leaf over onto the ventral side, it (the act of overturning) symbolizes the woman's desire of not having or conceiving any more children.

## 12. THE ANTICLOCK MOVEMENT

The fixing of the main pillars of the house starts with the fixing of the mothur med. The remaining pillars are fixed into the ground in an anticlock direction. This practice is observed because the Thakars believe that the sun and the whole cosmos move in an anticlockwise direction. Most rites which are performed to bring good fortune to the Thakars are performed in an anticlock movement. The rotation in such movements is also anticlock in direction. For instance, the moving of "tambya" in the diagnostic ritual, the dance movements, moving of the bride and the groom around the sacred fire also is done in the anticlock direction.

After fixing the four pillars in the four directions, a small wooden plank of the jamun tree (Eugenia Jambolina) is fixed in the center of the roof. It symbolizes the sky. A coconut is tied to this pole. the water in the coconut symbolizes the rain and the coconut the clouds. the Thakars worship the jamun pole (sky) during construction in the belief that doing so will prevent the house from leaking.

## THE THAKAR HOUSE AS A SYMBOL OF UNIVERSE

The culturally designed structure of the Thakar house is similar to their perception of the cosmos. The four pillars in the Thakar house are symbolic of the four directions. The first pillar symbolizes the sun. The ritual of fixing the mothur med into a hole dug by the males is symbolic of the origin of a family as it depicts the sexual relationship between the mother earth and the sun. (sun is believed to be the husband of the earth). The offering of the coconut by the males symbolizes the spermatic flow of the sun into the earth.

The horizontal jamun pole (Engenia jambolina) symbolizes the sky. The coconut hung on the "Aada"- the jamun plank symbolizes the clouds and the water in it symbolizes the rain. The offering of a coconut by the Thakar is an appeal to the sky not to let the roof leak.

The three directions, north, west and east are believed to bring the life giving air, while the south is believed to be evil and brings trouble, illness and death to the Thakars. The anticlock direction followed during building a house by fixing the poles in symbolic of the anticlock movement of the Thakar Gods 'Sun' and his brother 'Moon'. Even other cosmic forces such as wind, clouds, seasons are believed to move in an anticlock direction. The Thakar house thus is a symbol of the cosmic outlook of the Thakars.

## The Human Body and the Cosmos

The Thakars categorize the human body into a universal whole. According to them the human body comprises of ten openings viz, the eyes, the nose, the mouth, the atma (the region below the sternum), pulse of wrist, the naval, the vaginal opening, the pulse of the feet and the anal opening . These ten openings symbolize the ten planets in the cosmos. The planets are similarly ordered like the openings in the body. The Thakars believe that just as the universe exists because of the sun. The Thakars believe that man is able to see because the sun supplies light to the eyes during the day and the moon supplies light at night.

The blood circulation is also anticlockwse in direction just like the movement of the cosmic objects and forces in the universe. The body survives because of

1. Light: The source is the sun and the moon.
2. Water: Believed to be the brother of the sun and the source is clouds and earth.
3. Wind: Comes/blows from north, east and west directions.
4. Food: Made up of earth, sun and water.

The Thakar defines life within this framework and therefore the body is closely related to the universe. Due to this close association the "Baya" (cosmic Goddesses) visited Mrs. Dharma Pardhi and asked her to leave the A.D.S. the construction of which did not fit into the cultural framework of the Thakars.

### Reason for Mrs. Pardhi's illness and Troubles

Mrs. Dharma Pardhi thus attributed all her illness and troubles to the fact that they i.e. she, her husband and their children, did not live in a culturally designed house of the Thakars which resembles the human body and is a symbol of the universe. The order of the body and universe must be similar or should resemble in order to have perfect harmony.

This harmony was clearly absent in the A.D.S. house in which Mrs. Dharma Pardhi lived with her family.

Thus this illness episode cross-cuts meanings of many institutions such as material culture, cosmic perceptions, the notion of evil spirits, the concept of human body as a cosmic symbol etc.

## 3.8 Sacred spots in Tribal Houses

My experience of working with the tribals as a researcher and development expert for last years helped me to reach to a conclusion that in every tribal culture there are sacred spots and/ or places. Secondly during rituals of transition, most tribal groups have specific spots or points in a house which are used for the rituals. Given below are tribewise few examples.

**Table No. 3.1: Tribewise sacred spots in tribal houses**

| Sr. No. | Tribe | Spot | Ritual Associated with it |
|---|---|---|---|
| 1. | Warli | Ukhali (Hollow and circular stone groove used for pounding) | On the 3rd day of the wedding among the warlis, the bride's aunt's draw a figure of a flower around the pounding hole with rice powder, turmeric & kunku. This rectangular flowery figure with a multiplication sign on the pounding hole is called "Kanna" |

*(Contd...)*

| *1* | *2* | *3* | *4* |
|---|---|---|---|
| | | | This rectangular figure with across on the hole symbolizes the virginity of the bride. The groom's aunts erase this figure with cowdung & redraw another Kanna without the cross. The action of erasing the cross symbolizes first sexual intercourse. While the flowery figure is being erased the girl (bride) cries in pain. The loud crying symbolizes the breaking of hymen. During this ritual the parents, relatives and the villagers socially declare that the bride is a virgin. To conclude the "Ukhali" in wedding ritual setting becomes a significant spot, for the Warlis. |
| 2. | Kokna | Loft (Mala) | Bohada is a mask festival celebrated by Koknas. Every household keeps a mask called 'mukhavata' on the loft. It is covered with a cloth and kept in a basket, towards the eastern side of the loft. |
| 3. | Thakar | Topli | Thakars make a small basket in which a copper motif called "Tak", which is a symbol of ancestral spirits. The "Tak" is kept on the loft and is believed to be sacred. |
| 4. | Madia | Courtyard | Madias of Gadchiroli make a marriage pillar. This is a gift from a boy to his would be wife. The marriage pillar is kept in front of the house of the bride in case of arranged marriage. During this ritual the courtyard becomes a sacred place. |

Several such examples can be given from different tribal cultures. Architects who design tribal housing projects should take into account the cultural values attached to tribal housing designs.

## 3.9 Ecology And Tribal Housing Patterns

After analysing the house structures, their designs, the material used by the tribals to construct the houses is determined by the ecological environment in which the tribals live. Trees, shrubs, bamboos, creepers etc. found within an ecological setting contribute to housing material. The utility of these plants give them a sacred status in construction and or housing rituals. Table 3.2 throws light on showing how ecology shapes housing designs and patterns.

**Table No. 3.2: Tribewise Plants used for building a house**

| Sr.No. | Tribe | State/District | House material & Ecological speciality |
|---|---|---|---|
| 1. | Irula | Tamil Nadu | (a) *Roof*- Thatched roofs are made up of coconut palm leaves as coconut palms are available in abundance.<br>(b) *Walls*- Made up of mud. |
| 2. | Warli | Maharashtra (Konkan belt) | (a) *Roof*- Thatched roofs made up of rice stalks as rice is grown abundantly in Konkan region of Maharashtra state.<br>(b) *Walls*- Warlis make walls with Karvi sticks, as karvi is abundantly found in Konkan belt. |
| 3. | Naga | Nagaland | (a) *Roof*- Thatched roofs are made up of rice straw.<br>(b) *Walls*- Nagas use bamboos to make walls of their traditional house. Since bambo is available in abundance they use bamboos. |
| 4. | Bhils | Maharashtra Rajasthan Gujarat Madhya Pradesh | (a) *Roofs*- Thatched roof is made up of Jawar (millet) stalks as Jawar is grown abundantly in the geographical areas wherein Bhils dwell.<br>(b) *Walls*- Wall are either made up of bamboo sheets or clay. |
| 5. | Madias of Gadchiroli District in Maharashtra | | (a) *Roofs*- Thatched roofs are made up of rice stalks.<br>(b) *Walls*- House walls are made up of teak wood. The Madias build houses which are 3 to 4 feet above the ground level. This is to prevent a wild animals from entering the house. The compound too is made up of wooden poles so as to protect themselves from wild animals. |

Hence the flora available in the given environment, mobile nature of the tribe, socio-economic status, and sultural interpretation of house design are factors, that determine the tribal house patterns and designs. For example the Birhor tribe of Bihar is a mobile tribe and hence use bamboos and Butea frondosa leaves to cover their houses which are 5 x 5 feet in size. They are circular in shape. Similarly the Katkaris who migrate to work on brick kilns, live in small temporary brick huts, while they are away from their native places.

Yet another interesting aspect observed among tribal cultures in this regard is that, they classify certain plants as males while some as females. The Thakars classify Teak tree as a male plant and Jamun tree as a female plant. Hence for cetain rituals only male plants and others females.

## 3.10 Understanding tribal housing symbolism: An Imperative Need

Given the above background, it is imperative on the part of policy makers and implementers of tribal housing shcemes to understand the symbols and their meanings associated with house design, layout and construction. Unless & until an indepth study of tribal housing symbolism is done with the help of Anthropologists it will be difficult to plan housing projects for tribals. It is recommended that Anthropological inputs be considered prior to planning tribal housing projects.

After a detailed documentation is done with the help of Anthropologists, the next step is to call for people's participation and respect their views in planning, implementing and following up housing projects.

*****

# CHAPTER—4

# STATUS OF TRIBAL HOUSING SCHEME: AN OVERVIEW

## 4.1 Housing scheme

The Government of Maharashtra implements a housing schemes for the tribals in Maharashtra through the Panchayat Samiti (a block level development organization) of Zilla Parishad (the district level development agency). This housing scheme is known as Indira Awas Yojna or Gharkool Yojna. An attempt has been made by the researcher to assess the conditions and status of the houses built by the panchayat samiti for the tribals. The data has been presented in the form of case studies. Given below are the case studies which depicts the status, conditions, problems and positive aspects of the Indira awas and Gharkool housing yojna.

### CASE STUDY NO. 1

Jaisingh Valvi, age 46, a male, member of a Bhil tribe, and a resident of Nimboni village, in Navapur block of Nandurbar district, in the state of Maharashtra, India, built a house of his own. Instead of the traditional walls of bamboos smeared with clay, Jaisingh used bricks to make the walls of his new house. The thatched roof was replaced with cement sheets. The nine wooden pillars to support the traditional bamboo walls were replaced with bricks. The new house did not have wooden pillars. It had two doors, one (main) facing the North while the rear one was facing south. The Bhils of Nimboni don't let the doors of their houses face the west because the monsoon winds blow from the west. To avoid rain getting into the house Bhils avoid making a window door or a verandah facing the west.

The window of Jaisingh's new house was facing the north. The built up area of Jaisingh's new house was 20 by 25 feet, including a small verandah of 8 by 25 feet. When asked why was the house built according to the Bhil cultural traditions and customs? He gave following replies.

*(i)* **Rectangular Shape:** He maintained the traditional rectangular shape of the house.

*(ii)* **Verandah:** He made a verandah (plinth) as per the traditional norms.

*(iii)* **Direction Symbolism**: As per the Bhil traditions the doors were facing north and south, and not the west.

*(iv)* **Aada Pillar**: The central pillar of the roof which symbolises the sky and is traditionally made up of teak wood was replaced by an iron pillar. It was worshipped by a Bhil carpenter as per the cultural norms. A coconut was tied to it.

(v) **The North East**: The auspicious pillar (in this case) the brick built corner) was worshipped by the Head of the household Jaisingh and his wife, as per the Bhil tradition.

*(vi)* **The Fire Place at the South West**: Jaisingh did not forget to make small kitchen outside the main house and built "Chulah" - the fire place used for cooking food, at the south-western part of the house.

*(vii)* **Grain Storage**: Right in the middle of his main house he built a plinth of 2 x 4 feet long and two feet high to keep the bags of food grains on it. Traditionally he would store them in bamboo baskets called "Kangas".

*(viii)* **A Thatched Wall Bathroom**: Jaisingh built a squarish thatched wall bathroom without a door for the family members to take bath. The women folk use a sari curtain which seems as a door.

(ix) **The Floor**: The floor of the house was made up of clay, nicely plastered and smeared with cowdung as per the traditions

*(x)* **The Traditional Bhil House Lay out**: When asked how is the layout of the traditional Bhil house, Jaisingh draw a sketch which was as follows:

*(xi)* **Analysis**: Jaisingh's new house although was made up bricks, iron poles and cement sheets, yet it had the traditional architecture, layout and design. He performed all the traditional rituals as per the Bhil cultural norms. Psychologically both Jaisingh, his wife and his family members are at peace because they have followed all the traditions of constructing a Bhil house. That they are confident that no evil force or being will cast evil eye on their house, nor disturb their family peace.

To conclude, Jaisingh's case study is a classic example of how important it is for policy makers and implementers of housing schemes to understand and respect cultural traditions of a tribal community, before launching an intervention program. This was possible, because Jaisingh himself invested Rs. 50.000/-, supervised the construction process, involved key personnel from his community to plan, implement and monitor the construction process.

An informal discussion with Jai Singh revealed that he would wait for that day, when my hamlet gets all the facilities.

## Facilities in a Tribal Hamlet

*(a)* Primary school

*(b)* I.C.D.S unit

*(c)* Gram Panchayat office

*(d)* Samaj Mandir

*(e)* Clinic/Sub centre/Nurse

*(f)* Pada Workers Unit

*(g)* Water tank for animals

(h) Vetenery

(i) Wells-2 (irrigation)

(j) Bathroom/Toilets with water/Taps.

(k) Chavdi

(l) Hand pumps 3 to 4

(m) Electricity in every house

(n) Flour mill

(o) Shop

(p) Fair price shop

(q) Roads to the village

(r) Grain Bank unit for every hamlet

(s) Agriculture unit/Training centre

— Seeds centre

— Fertilisers centre

— Spray centre

— Guidance centre

— Oil engine/Electric pump

## CASE STUDY NO. 2

Moru Hari Thorad, age 36, a male, member of Thakar Tribe, and a resident of Nagewadi hamlet, of pathraj village, of karjat block in Raigad district, from the state of Maharashtra, India. Moru was a beneficiary of the Government Housing Scheme called "gharkool scheme", during the financial year 2002 to 2003.

Although the scheme was sanctioned by the "Panchayat Samiti"-a block level development agency, Moru made it a point to build the house as per the Thakar cultural norms. The panchayat samiti sanctioned a sum of Rs. 28,500/- for building Moru's house. This was certainly great help to Moru and his family. Moru spend another 5,000/- rupees to get cement for plastering the walls. The process of planning, implementing and monitoring the house construction was as follows:

*(i)* **Site selection**: Moru Thorad, requested his brother Walku Hari Thorad - a shaman to investigate the plot of land on which he was going to build his house. Walku performed traditional rituals to identify if there was any evil force or being on the land. Walku performed the diagnosis ritual by rotating a metal pot filled with water in a clockwise (in auspicious) direction and put ash (the body of Sun) in the pot and found that the water was clear. Ash did not float on the water. Walku the shaman gave green signal to his brother Moru by saying that the land selected for constructing the house was good and there was no evil hinderance.

*(ii)* **Squarish shape**: Moru maintained the squarish shape of his house as per the traditional Thakar cultural norms.

*(iii)* **Doors:** Moru just made one door facing the North. Among the Thakars they do not face their house doors towards the South. The doors may face East, West and North.

*(iv)* **Aada pillar**: The central pillar of the roof which symbolises the sky and is traditionally made up of teak wood. It was worshipped by a Thakar carpenter. A coconut was tied in a cloth so as to appease the God of rains to prevent the roof from leaking.

*(v)* **The South-East**: The auspicious pillar (in this case the brick built corner) was worshipped by fire Thakar males including Moru - the head of the new house. Traditionally five Thakar men would insert a teak wooden pillar in the hole. The insertion of the pillar in the hole symbolises the sexual union of the Sun with mother Earth. This establishes a family. Moru worshipped the brick pillar in the Southeast.

*(vi)* **The fire place at the South east**: Thakars compulsorily build the hearth (stove) - the cooking place next to the pillar (mothur med) at the south-east corner, as per their traditions. Fire is considered to be Goddess 'hole'

by the Thakars. She is the sister of Sun on Earth. Fire contributes in cooking and hence survival of human beings. Fire therefore is an element linked with survival.

*(vii)* **Anticlock building of pillars and walls**: Traditionally the Thakars first insert the 'mothur med' - wooden pillar at the south-east corner of their squarish shaped house. Then in an anticlock manner insert the remaining three poles. Keeping the auspicious anticlock movement in view, moru did build the four brick pillars in an anticlock manner. The walls too were built in that manner. This completed the traditional ritual.

*(viii)* **Back yard and Court yard**: Moru left 1000 sq. feet space both in front and back of his house respectively, as per the traditions norms. Thakars use the front court yard for threshing rice, while the back yard is used as a kitchen garden.

*(ix)* **Loft**: Moru saw to it that a loft was built to store food grains, seeds, etc.

*(x)* **Ukhali**: A pounding hole which is used for seperately husk from rice grains was made in the living room.

### Concluding Remarks

Although Government of Maharashtra funded the housing project of Moru Thorad. Moru took personal interest in seeing that the modern process of construction fits into the traditional norms of building a Thakars house.

## CASE STUDY NO. 3

### (1) Aim of the case study

To analyse the views of Thakars regarding the Indira Awas Housing Yojna.

### (2) Background

The Indira Awas Housing Yojna was named after the name of the late Prime Minister of India, Mrs Indira Gandhi. The aim of the scheme was to provide housing to the weaker section of the Indian society, including the members of scheduled tribes and castes. The budget of this scheme per house was

However, while constructing the houses people were not taken into confidence and their views regarding how the house should be built was not taken into account. This case study presents how a tribal community did not take advantage of this scheme because its members were not involved in planning, implementation, and monitoring of this scheme.

### (3) Course of events

Nagewadi is a hamlet exclusively inhabited by the Thakar tribe, in pathraj village of Karjat tahsil in Raigad district of Maharashtra. The panchayat samiti implemented the Indira Awas Yojna for four families during the year,1996-97. There were houses in a row having tin sheet roofs. The built up space of every house was just 200 sq. feet. The doors were facing south. The construction was no where close to traditional Thakar housing style. Hence all the four families did not live in there houses.

One of the member of the Thorad family used the house for storing fire wood. While the other three families used the three houses for storing rice strawand fodder for the cattle.

### (4) Concluding Remarks

Since the design and layout of the Indira Awas housing was no where close to Thakar concept of house designs, its beneficiaries (Thakars) did not make use of these houses. The beneficiaries said they were better off in their traditional houses made up stick walls, thatched roofs with enough space for their family members and cattle as well.

## CASE STUDY NO. 4

### (1) Aim of the case study

To study why some tribes choose to live in houses built by the Government, although these houses are not built as per their traditional cultural norms.

### (2) Background

Ramwadi is a small hamlet of Katkari tribe, of Kotimbe village in Karjat tahsil of Raigad district in Maharashtra state. There are 44 families who have been given houses under the Indira Awas Yojna. These houses were not build as per the cultural norms of the Katkaris. As far as size of the houses are concerned, they are small, without light, and the material used for construction is not up to the mark.

On enquiring about why they still persist to live in those houses most of them said we have no option. We are landless and daily wage labourers, we can not afford to build a house of our own. Hence, some thing is better than nothing.

### (3) Analysis

It is not the Katkaris alone who go through such a situation. There are several landless and daily wage labourers - members of other tribes in India have no option but to choose to live in such houses. They blame it on their fate.

## CASE STUDY NO. 5

### (1) Aim of the case study

To explore the factors responsible for planning, implementing and follow-up of toilet scheme in a tribal village.

### (2) Background

Several tribal villages in Nandurbar have been given toilets. The objective behind giving toilets to tribal family from an outsider's point was good and scientific, but the tribals had another argument altogether.

### (3) The scheme

A toilet of 4′ x 4′ feet was provided to a tribal family. The hight of the same was eight feet high. An eastern commode was fixed in the centre. Each toilet was suppose to have a door. The quality of bricks and cement used for constructing this was not up to the mark.

The gram sevak (village level Government Development Officer) implemented this scheme for the Zilla Parishad (District Development Agency). He never planned the scheme with the people, nor asked for their views. The toilets were built without involving people in planning. As per the information given to us by the Bhil tribals of Dhekvad and Nimboni villages in Nandurbar and Navapur blocks of Nandurbar districts the Government had spent Rs. 5,000/- on each toilets. In Dhekvad village about 110 toilets were built about 6-7 years ago, while in Nimboni 60 toilets were built.

### (4) Impact of the Scheme

After 7 long years when we went to evaluate the impact of the scheme. We observed that only two households out of 110 in Dhekwad and 4 households out 60 families in Nimboni were using the toilet.

The rest of the tribal families put a stone tablet over the commode and started using the toilet as a bathroom for taking bath. They also used it for washing clothes.

### (5) Reasons for Failure of the Scheme

An in-depth and informal dialogue with the tribals of Dekhvad and Nimboni mostly Bhils and Koknas it was observed that the reasons for the failure were as follows:

*(a)* **Lack of planning**: Government officials never bothered to plan the scheme with the beneficiaries (tribals) for whom the scheme was to be implemented.

*(b)* **No prior research for survey**: No efforts were made to document the views of tribals regarding the scheme, nor their habits and behaviour regarding defecation was explored.

*(c)* **No training and education**: Beneficiaries were not educated or trained before implementing the scheme. Tribals are used to go out in the bushes, fields and forests for defecation. They finish up their morning duties before the sunrise. Men and women have separate defecation grounds. They either use leaves

or stones after they defecate. Most tribals do not use water after defecation like the Hindus do. Since most of the villagers were used to going out in the fields for defecation they did not use the toilets.

*(d)* **Position of the built toilet**: The gram sevak gave orders to build the toilets where ever space was found. Some toilets were built right in front of the house, i.e. in the front courtyard. Guests of the tribals come and sit on the verandah in front of the house. The users as well as the visitors would have felt very embarrassing. The smell of the toilet could have created further problems.

*(e)* **No water source**: Not a single toilet was provided with a water tank or tap/pipe line. This meant toilet without water (no flushing) would have led to further menace. Secondly no training was given to the tribals about clearing and toilet maintenance. They were not aware of the different types of brushes and toilet cleaners used to clean the toilets.

### (6) Analysis

From the above course of events related to the foilet scheme for the tribals it is clear that unless and until prior research is done, a community is organised in order to call for its participation, unless people are educated and trained, the efforts to implement programs like the one narrated in this case study are futile. This is a classic example of how Government resources are wasted.

## CASE STUDY NO. 6

### (1) Aim of the case study

To highlight the negligence in follow-up of Indira awas housing scheme for the Katkaris.

### (2) Background

Shitul wadi is a tribal hamlet inhabited exclusively by the Katkari tribe. This hamlet is situated about 6 to 7 Kms away from 'Pen' - the tahsil head quarters, which also happens to be the head quarter of the project officer Tribal Development. There are altogether 60 houses in this village. As per the information given by the villagers 47 houses were constructed under the Indira awas housing scheme, 10 houses under the new "Gharkool" sheme, while only 3 houses have been built by the Katkaris themselves.

It was observed that the 3 personal houses built by the Katkaries and 10 Gharkool yojna houses built by the Zilla parishad were good as compared to the 47, built under the Indira awas yojna.

### (3) What went wrong?

After inspecting and carefully observing the condition of the houses it was observed that:

*(a)* **The construction quality**: The construction quality of the Indira awas housing shceme were not up to the mark.

*(b)* **Material used**: The material used for constructing such as cement, bricks, clay, wood etc too was sub-standard. Due to this reason even a slight pressure on the walls would remove the plaster.

Instead using cement the Government constructors who built these houses had used clay in between the bricks. The material used for external plastering had less cement and more sand, because of which a slight pressure or knock on the wall would remove the plaster. I felt that the quality of construction was poor.

### (4) Other Problems

Mangalya Janya Katkari, who was promised a house, was never given one. He has built a stone plinth and has bought few bricks but he is still waiting for the day when he will get a house. Currently he is staying with his son-in-law. Mangalya told us that in our culture a father-in-law never stays with a son-in-law. My poverty has forced me to do that. What will I do if my son-in-law throws me out of his house? Well, Mangalya has to wait for his turn.

Even with the houses built under the "Gharkool" yojna there were few problems. These were:

*(a)* Clay was used in between the bricks, instead of cement.

(b) External part of the house was plastered with cement while the internal wall did not has cement at all.

(c) These four houses were built in a row, instead of building them separately. By doing this expense of building an extra wall was saved by the contractor.

(d) Height of some houses was very low. This too meant that the contractor saved material and money.

(e) Not a single beneficiary out of the 13, knew about, how much amount was sanctioned for their house. All that they did was to sign the bank slip for the "gram sevak" (Village Development Officer).

### (5) Analysis

Implementers of the Indira awas and Gharkool programs taken advantage of the ignorance, illiteracy, and poverty of the Katkaris and cheat them. Its time to check the corruption at grass root level linked with tribal housing.

## CASE STUDY NO. 7

### (1) Aims of the case study

To explore the efforts made by an N.G.O to construct houses for a Katkari village.

### (2) Background

Khairaswadi is a Katkari hamlet situated about 13 kms away from 'Pen' its tahsil head quarters. Although it is close to a town, it is an inaccessible village, because there is no proper approach road to the village. It is situated on the mountain, away from the main village . The Katkaris walk 8 kms to get drinking water from a village pond. This water is not chlorinated. We took a survey of this village and found out that almost 100% of the villagers do not boil water before drinking. Most of the villagers suffer from water borne diseases. The nearest clinic and Health Centre is 8 kms away from the village. The primary Health Centre staff hesitate to go to this village as there is no bus nor rikshaw service to this village.

It was possible for us to go this village because we borrowed the Jeep of the project officer Tribal Development, Pen. Given the background of this hamlet no one would want to go and do some development work. Hats off to the "Dalmiya Seva Trust" an N. G. O. from Bombay, which has started some good work in this village.

### (3) Efforts by Dalmiya Seva Trust

Dalmiya Seva Trust is an N. G. O. based in Bombay. This organisations efforts in Khairaswadi are worth mentioning. These are:

*(a)* **Housing project**: The Dalmiya Seva Trust has built brick houses for all the Katkaris of Khairaswadi. These houses are good as compared to the houses built under Indira Awas and Gharkool Yojna.

*(b)* **School building**: The same N. G. O. has build a school for the Katkari children. It is upto 4th grade. A teacher from the neighbouring village manages it.

*(c)* **Health Camps**: The N. G. O. also organises health camps in this village.

*(d)* **Immunisation camp base**: The school building built by the Dalmiya Seva Trust is used a base for immunising Katkari children and women, by the primary Health Centre staff.

### (4) Analysis

There are several N. G. O's like the Dalmiya Seva Trust who are involved in social service of the tribals and more importantly the landless and poor katkaris. Government fund such N. G. O's to carry out housing projects.

## CASE STUDY NO. 8

### (1) Aim of the case study

To highlight the status of tribal houses at the brick kilns.

### (2) Background

Brick industry in India has gained significance since 1970's because of high rising demand for ownership flats in the cities, towns as well as in some rural areas. Besides ownership flats there are constructions of other types as well. The supply of bricks to the construction company from the brick kiln owners.

The brick kiln owners are usually landlords who exploit the weaker sections of the Indian Society namely the landless tribes and the members of the Scheduled Castes. The brick kiln owners employ the poor tribals and members of scheduled castes at a very low wages. The brick kiln labourers work from Oct. to May.

Katkari tribe is one group involved as a labour force in the Brick Industry. The owner pays each family a sum of Rs. 3,000/- on an average per month, but extracts a profit of Rs. 50,000/- to one lakh, from one family. This is disgraceful, economic transaction studies by Bhatia Arun and Tribhuwan Robin have revealed that over 98% of the brick kiln Katkari labourers borrow money from their owners for survival during the rainy season. This borrowing forces them to go back to the brick kilns and get exploited.

### (3) Conditions of the Katkari Houses

For six months the brick kiln labourers live in small temporary houses made at the brick kiln site. The area of a nuclear family's house at the brick kiln site varies from 50 to 100 square feet. The hight of the walls is hardly four feet to six feet. Walls are nothing but piled up bricks. The roof constitutes of wooden sticks on which rice straw is kept.

These houses are not comfortable for living at all, but the poor and helpless Katkaris have to pull on along with their kids for six long months. It is extremely cold from October to January. and extremely hod from March to May. While the parents are at work children are left to the mercy of mother nature. These houses have no doors, hence snakes, insects, dogs, cats, rats, scorpions find their way in easily. Snake bites and scorpion stings are often reported.

### (4) Analysis

The Government authorities must intervene and pressurise the brick kiln owners to build good houses for their labourers. They must be legally taken to task as regards low payments made by them to the labourers. More importantly the housing projects need to be promoted either by the owners or by Government.

## CASE STUDY NO. 9

### (1) Aim of the case study

To highlight the status of tribal houses who work as sugar cane cutters.

### (2) Background

Western Maharashtra is known for sugar cane production. Rich farmers who are also in active politics have established sugar factories. The chairman of these factories have infact created a new political lobby, popularly known as 'sugar lobby'. These politicians have given "birth" a middleman - the contractors who hire cheap labour from tribal areas as well as famine struck districts. Most of the sugar cane cutters are landless and hence opt to be exploited along with their family members.

The Bhils of Dhule and Nandurbar who are landless have started migrating temporarily for six months to the sugar cane fields as labourers. The middlemen take them in tractors or trucks to the sugar cane fields. They have to cut the sugar cane, pile it in a truck and then go to the sugar factory to unload the same. These labourers work from 12 to 17 hours a day. In return for their hard work they get Rs. 2,000 to 3,000 per month.

### (3) Condition of their houses

As compared to the brick kiln labourers, the sugar cane workers live in worse houses. Their houses are very small from 40 to 50 square feet made up of sugar cane stalks, in a conical shape more or less that of the red indian houses. These houses are not good at all to live in. The Bhils, however have to live as there is no option.

### (4) Analysis

A serious thought needs to be given to the housing issues of the sugar cane workers who spend 3 to 6 moths on the farms with their children without good health, water, sanitary etc facilities.

Their children often become victims of diarrhoea, dysentery, gastro. Hence a serious thought needs to be given to millions of sugar cane workers whose life is controlled by the sugar cane lobby and the middlemen.

## CASE STUDY NO. 10

### (1) Aim of the case study

To explore the village and house patterns, construction procedures, and rituals associated with Naga house construction.

### (2) Background

"Abode of the Highlanders", the cultural realm of Haga has been known by many names. All convey a sense of remoteness, seclusion and isolation, in which there is doubtless some truth. Geographically the Naga cultural recalm of Naga is exclusively mountainous region formed when the Indian sub-continental plate thrust up beneath the Eurasian plate some 50 million years ago, creating the mighty Himalayas (Ham peter & Stirn Aglaya 2003). Nagas as the name suggest is a major tribe of Nagaland - a North-eastern state of India. The Nagas have several sub-tribes namely AO, Rengma, Seema, Angami etc. Being a highlander tribe most of them live on high mountains and hills in donse forests. They depend on forest for survival. Most of their housing resources and material comes from the forest. Housing is very closely related to ecology. Nagas build their houses on a board of teak wooden poles and bamboos about 6 to 8 feet above the ground. This is to prevent wild animals from entering the houses. This case study presents a cultural profile of naga housing patterns and the rituals associated with construction. The research work of Aglaja stirn and Peter Van Ham (2003: 54 to 63) on the Naga house patterns and rituals associated with it is reported here in this case study.

### (3) The Naga are hill-dwellers

Occupying hilltops or the highest possible points along a hill slope, reaching almost any of their villages is an arduous task. This settlement pattern is largely a result of the custom of headhunting, formerly prevalent throughout the Naga cultural realm. Inter-village feuds being frequent, it was necessary to situate villages out of reach of raiding parties. Hilltops, of course, provide ideal vantage points for detecting enemy activities or imminent attack. Yet other considerations also influenced the siting of Naga villagea, for instance, climatc. Bclow 500 m the climate is hot and unhealthy; above 1,500 m it is unpleasantly cold in winter and, during the monsoon, cloud is perpetual. Abundant springs are frequent above 1,500 m and water tends to be scarce. Despite this, several villages of the Chang, Khiamniungan and the Yimchunger are situated well above 1,500 m.

Villages came by their names in various ways. A local feature or site pecularity might be taken; the Nocte village of Lothong, for instance, refers to its palm leaf grove situation. 'The name of the Rengma village of Tesophebyu drives from when the jungle was cleared to build the village and a great number of black ants (teso) appeared. The Rengma took this as a favourable sign. The Chakhesang village name of Dzulhami comes from "dzu"(water), "lha" (spread) and "ml" (inhabitants). The Ao village name "Mopungchukit" means "where the wind rests" - it is related that when certain Ao were driven from longkhum by a village fire, the wind blew a plam leaf from a burning roof; where the leaf came to rest was taken as the site of the new village. The Angami village of Kidima means "big house", so named because of its inhabitants' large houses. The Sema generally name their villages after their chiefs or after village founders.

## (4) Village Patterns of the Nagas

Naga village patterns differ from group to group, ranging from no self-evident pattern to strict arrangements that can assume an almost terrace-house character. Thus the Ao and Lhota arrange their houses along regular streets, often along ridge tops. Chang settlements are similar. Tuensang with its four village quarters is built along winding, stone-paved lanes, reminiscent of a medieval town. Stone paths are a unique feature of some Konyak villages. Constructed for the monsoon period, they divide village quarters, or lead to important village-sites and often have magic-symbolic associations.

No two villages are alike. In some, houses are grouped together in a compact block and enclosed by a fence or stockade; in others they may be scattered in clusters, interspersed with vegetable plots and bamboo groves. Where level ground is scares, groups of dwellings may stand on different levels, even separated by gorges and broken grounds. Among the Kaiyaw it was common to build houses so close that their eaves touched. The Tangsas build their houses on hill slopes, one above the other in an orderly manner. Anami and Chakhesang houses, though irregualr, are generally built in two rows, the fronts facing east, the gable ends of each row of houses projecting towards a street. This is promoted by the traditional belief that after death the soul wanders westwards to the land of the dead. In many southern villages houses are surrounded by stone walls forming compounds where cattle are kept at night. Among the Zeliangrong of Cachar it was common to move village every four or five years because of the difficult terrain and limited workable land. This was also true of some Naga group in Myanmar such as the southern Haime, although their moves had more to do with deprivation, or the demands of other Naga groups and Jingphaw invasions.

### (5) House Patterns and Construction

Most Naga houses contain a central living space where the family sleeps, eats and lives, plus an entrance area, in which guests are greeted and entertained. Porches, anterooms and storage areas supplement the central core, their exact number and sequence depending on group and, sometimes, a family's financial status. There are three basic types of house: earth floor, earth and raised floor, and raised floor only, the later being found among the northern Naga groups such as the Nocte, Tutsa and Tangsa. The first style extends to almost all southern groups and also occurs among the Lower Konyak and Wancho. The second style, where the living are or a portion of it is raised above ground level, is found level, is found among all the central Naga groups. The Lhota, who may have adopted this from the Ao, cover the raised floor with earth, while others use woven bamboo slats and mats. Such features dictate a dwelling's appearance; southern groups favour a simple layout with a barn-like double pitched roof and plain gable end. While precise in shape, the extension of front eaves and size vary, the basic design being the same throughout the area. In houses where the floor is earth and raised, the earth part is normally located at the front where the rice pounder is kept; the living quarters are raised and extend to a platform at the rear where tasks such as weaving are performed.

The interior of a Naga house is 3-5 m from floor to ridge, though Rengma houses are considerably lower. A good part of this hight, especially the above the fireplaces, is used for storing provisions in swing-like racks that hang from the celling. These racks are also used for smoking new baskets to make them more durable.

Naga houses having no windows, the only light in an otherwise pitch dark interior comes through the cracks in the bamboo walls and from the fire. Nor are there any chimneys or ventilation holes for the smoke to escape through, so soot gradually covers the entire interior; this, naturally, makes the dwelling seem even darker; it also contributes to the inhabitants' relatively low life expectancy. Houses often catch fire. The spirit responsibel for a fire must be appeased by the shaman in a ritual during which the family shelters in a neighbouring house. Only after a certain genna period may reconstruction begin.

### (6) Rituals Associated with House Construction

After the erection of the main posts and beams it takes two to three days to complete a building. The owner gives every worker a free meal each day, serving rice beer at regular intervals. Traditional house construction was swift since owners were anxious to move in before an evil spirit could, often as soon as one or two walls were standing and the roof in place. Among the Maram it was common, when the house was partly habitable, for the owner to enter with a spear, s shield, a live cock and burning wood to chase away any evil spirits. A male friend assisted in lighting the first family fire at the three-stoned hearth to the right to the door. From this day - "the day of housewarming" - the fire had to be kept going for the next five days. The family entered the house on the first evening and would prepare a meal from the sacrificial cock.

If the house to be constructed was a chief's then the rituals and taboos among the Maram were more elaborate by far - a freshly hunted human head, for instance, was obligatory, the hunting of which was carried out by all male villagers. Failing a head, a little human hair at least from an unfriendly village had to be procured. Customs have changed, yet the sacrifice of a wild animal, preferably a tiger, is still required. Among the Tanga dog sacrifices were customary.

While a chief's house is being built the entire village is genna- no one may work in the fields, and commodities like rice, vegetables, cattle or poultry may not enter or leave the village, whether sold or as gifts. As soon as the main pillar and beam are up the chief starts a three-stage ceremony spread over a year. One of the cows must be black- which may mean procuring it from outside the village. It is killed first and specific ritual meanings attach to certain of its bodily parts. The right leg is sacrificed to Sarai, the God/Creator. Part of the hoof, ear, tongue and tail are laid on a banana leaf, wrapped up and doused in rice beer before being hung in the back of the house. Similar offerings are made to the village ancestors.

Stage two of the ritual takes place in September. The chief gathers as many men as possible to collect firewood with him and entertains them with special rice beer. The third stage takes place at harvest time, when the chief once more entertain his people with food and drink, this time also feeding the villages.

## (7) Khels and Morungs

Naga villages are usually divided into two or more khels (quarters, wards), depending on size and population; at times there are as many as eight, as in the Gongvan village of Tsawlaw. In some villages a khel is inhabited exclusively by members of a particular clan claiming descent from a common ancestor and naming their khel accordingly. Inter-clean rivalries were frequent. A clan inhabiting a certain khel was often closer to another village than to its immediate neighbours. In the late 19th century, for instance, neighbours of the Putchatsuma quarter in Kohima allowed Angami from Mozema to enter the quarter and take the heads of all present; the people of other Kohima khels looked on and made no attempt to interfere. Such circumstances led villages not only to be defensively situated but also fortified - when stone walls, bamboo spikes, wooden gates and a perimeter ditch. In general village attachments are strong, particularly towards main or parent villages, and generally people only leave the later when available land is insufficient for the population. Then settlements are established in areas with sufficient land to accommodate a new village. Relations to the original parent village may be reflected in the village name, e.g. the Wancho village of Chanu, where "nu" means mother, and Chasa where "sa" means son.

The centre of each khel is the morung (Wancho: pa, Nocte: poh, Phom: bang, Chang: Haki, Pochuri: awikhu, Ao: archu, Lhota: champo). This remarkable and most prominent house in the village gives visual, institutional and architectural expression to the solidarity of clan members. Morung architecture is not less diverse than the general architecture of different Naga groups. However, with the exception of the southern Naga groups who consider feast-givers' and chiefs' houses as particularly worthy of artistic attention, it is the morungs on which the most embellishment and care are lavished. This may be through its size, its woodcarvings, or any other special decoration such as front rafters from which fronds of grass or cane are hung (e.g. Khiamniungan, Lainong), or suspended fetishes signifying a village genna or any other significant message (e.g. Phom, Yimchunge). Apart from serving as guard-houses and as storage for all the village's weapons, it was here that males from around eight years to marrying age dwelt. Hence, boys were educated by older housemates in everything of importance for personal and communal life in village society.

Although Christianity has seen to it that schools have replaced the most comprehensive educational function of the morungs, they are nevertheless where elements of traditional Naga heritage such as the arts of weaving, costume-adornment, dancing, oral traditions, but also hunting skills and techniques of traditional warfare, are passed on to society's younger members. Hence these community houses remain the social focus of every village. While morungs are only rarely used now as adolescent dormitories, they are still meeting places and reception and entertainment houses for guests. Important decisions are often taken there. Naga student clubs and federations in particular are actively reviving morungs as foci of culture and art. Their social aspect is also being stressed again, being places where the old and sick and those without a family used to be cared for.

As institutional village centres morungs were ideal focal points for attackers. Those who controlled the morung controlled people. Apart from the innumerable clashes between Naga underground groups and the Indian Army, the burning of morungs instigated by Christian influence brought irreparable losses to the Naga cultural heritage. It is not far-fetched to compare the Naga morung with what the Western church stood for in the Middle Ages. It was held sacrosanct. Often it housed the skulls of slain enemies, in which the essential fertile power was thought to reside. Here the sacred anthologies of clans were recited and important religious rituals held. The persecuted found shelter in the morung, taking advantage of the inviolable custom of asylum within its bounds.

A morung's function, among some groups, was sometimes restricted to being a meeting place for village elders or the house in which the sacred log drum was stored. Among such groups, children are nevertheless still separated from their parents at an early age, sleeping either in a separate dormitory, an extension of the chief's house, or living with relatives or rich members of the community who sometimes put aside a room for the purpose.

### (8) Rationale of the Morung

Various theories have been put forward as to why the morung system came into being. One idea is that among groups without morungs the frequency of violent father/son quarrels increases. Not that disciplinary problems and generation crises are banished entirely of male adolescents are not at home. Yet the pressure is alleviated within the family, and crises, being acted out at a communal level, may arguably be more efficiently channelled than when a single person, the father, demands, say, behavioural changes from a son. For the individual concerned, seeing that no less is expected of anyone else, an understanding as to why certain behaviours are considered desirable may conceivably develop more easily. Yet character-shaping in traditional Naga could be rather drastic, as evident in the thick cane rings still suspended from morung ceilings among Ao and Phom. Disobedient morung members were apparently tied to these and hung over the fireplace until they showed willingness to comply.

An alternative, fundamentally freudian theory is that the morung system prevented children from witnessing the "primal scene", that is, the sexual act between parents. To much counter-evidence renders this thesis unacceptable, yet there sibling relations were indeed more frequent which, in the long run, might pose a serious threat to clan survival. Any form of incest is subject to the strongest social taboo in the various Naga societies today. It is known of the Minyong Adi - a tribal group living north of the Brahmaputra in Arunachal Pradesh and related to the Naga, that the femal morung (in their society called rasheng) arose in order to control sexual activity and channel it according to approved tribal laws and codes of conduct focusing on decency and enlightement.

### (9) Love Houses and Girls' Dormitories

Comparable customs are attested to in many Naga groups, most of which also have morungs for girls (Ao: zuki, Rengma: Katsen, Nocte: Yampo, Phom: yow). These girls' dormitories do not enjoy the same sacrosanct status as the morungs. They lack elaborate decoration, occupying secluded - rather than prominent geographical sites known only to other village inhabitants. Educationally, they are where girls learn everything to do with household and agricultural affairs, as well as the art of singing and dancing, while, publicly speaking, they function mainly as meeting places for young couples, married and unmarried (among the Nocte it is customary for newly-weds to stay in the yampo until one or two children have been born). So-called "love-houses" are also known from certain Burmese Naga groups - one example in Tsawlaw Naukkon was reported to have some thirty cubicles for couples.

Admission to the girls' dormitory takes place when a girl reaches puberty. While not so well organized as the morungs, girls' dormitories adhere strictly to their own age-group stipulations.

There are basically two categories of members - those with official lovers with whom they associate and sleep in the dormitory, and those who have no official boyfriend, consorting with any morung boys they please. Each couple sleeps side by side under a rug. As long as the sexual act is not seen, decency and decorum are not considered to be violated. Only unmarried girls can have such relationships. While the Naga are very clan and origin conscious and such behaviour counters exogamous group rules, it is not always possible to prevent sexual union between clan members in the girls' dormitories. A blind eye is generally turned to such relationships. Any pregnancy, however, is treated as severe offence, rendering a couple liable to a heavy fine, even "excommunication" in the case of a second pregnancy. Premarital conception is generally frowned on, even between members of different clans, although if the couple marries it becomes acceptable. While no definite social stigma falls on a girl conceiving under such circumstances and not marrying, certain plants' bark, leaves and roots are taken to induce abortion. Such drugs must be used clandestinely, however, as destruction of foetal life is culpable according to customary Naga Law.

### (10) Analysis

This case study has been a description of how the Naga tribe view their world of house construction, their settlement patterns and houses of socio-cultural significance such as youth dormitories, morungs and so on. It highlights how Naga cultural symbols and meanings are intertwined with house construction of the tribe. The case study should remind the policy makers to respect peoples cultural values associated with house construction. It also unveils the diversity and variety of rituals each tribe has about house construction.

## CASE STUDY NO. 11

### (1) Aim of the case study

To highlight houses of social significance Among the Indian tribes.

### (2) Background

Cultural solidarity is one of the significant trait of tribal communities world over. There are more community rituals in tribal societies than other societies. They have certain areas such as burial grounds - exclusively used for burying the dead. Like wise, there are places for the village Gods, apprenticeship of a shaman, village council etc. Some times they meet in open places, but sometimes there are special huts or houses wherein such social events are housed. this case study puts forth a few of those.

### (3) Ghotul

Ghotul is a youth dormitory of the "Madia" tribe. Ghotul is a hall in every "Madia" village wherein young boys and girls who attain puberty spend time. They find their boy friends as well as girl friends here. If a boy likes a girl he presents her a wooden comb called "Hichadi". The comb is a symbol of engagement ring. After, this the boy makes a 'marriage pillar' for her. This wooden pillar on which he carves images of flowers and ornaments is presented by him to his girl friend. The pillar is kept in front of the Ghotul. It is removed only when one of them dies.

Thus, Ghotul is an important house for the Madias. It is a place where they learn to sing, dance, play musical instruments and learn several aspects of their own culture. As an Anthropologist, I would categorise a 'Ghotul' as a platform for enculturation and socialisation. It is here that an youth learns about how to live within his society.

The point I am trying to make here is that while planning housing program for the Madia one needs to bear in mind Ghotul the youth dormitory.

### (4) Kurmi

Outside every Madia village is a small hut called Kurmi. When a woman delivers a child she is in a Kurmi. She only has a midwife with her. other than these two women no one from the village goes to the Kurmi. A new mother is allowed to come o her own house only after seven days. Even the father of the child is not allowed in the Kurmi for seven days.

When the Madia women get menstrual periods they live in the Kurmi's for a period of 3 to 5 days. She is given admission in her own house after she takes a bath. Kurmis are therefore very special to the Madias.

After an informal enquiry into the behaviour of shifting a woman from her family atmosphere to the Kurmi, it was observed, that menstrual blood according the Madias is impure and pollutes social environment, hence menstruating women are socially dislocated for 3 to 5 days. Hence a menstruating woman is made to let her blood out in the Kurmi.

The Madias associate cultural significance to the Ghotul and Kurmi, hence while planning housing project for a Madia settlement it is necessary to keep in mind these aspects.

### (5) Gotha (Manger)

It is observed that in most tribal societies of India cattle are tied with in the house or outside in a small house or courtyard. Among some tribes of Maharashtra cattle are tied outside their houses in small huts made up of stick walls and rice straw thatched roofs. Depending on the cultural norms and direction symbolism a Gotha is built. These aspects too need to be explored before planning settlements for tribals.

### (6) Analysis

Every tribe in India has a sacred place, a house for cattle, social gathering, meetings, love houses, youth dormitories etc. An in-depth understanding of tribal settlement pattern needs to be done before planning a tribal housing projects.

## CASE STUDY NO. 12

### (1) Aim of the Case Study

To explore the important places, spots and cultural occasions selected by the Gonds, Rathwas, Bhils, Suoras and Worlis to draw traditional paintings in certain spots on certain cultural occasions and events.

### (2) Background

In their book captioned "Threads Together: A study of Tribal and prehistoric paintings" Dr. Tribhuwan Robin and Finkenauer Maike (2003) have presented the cultural symbolism associated with the painting cults of Rathwa, Bhils, Gonds, Soara and Warli tribes from Gujarat, Madhya Pradesh, Orissa, and Maharashtra

**Table No. 4.1: Tribal paintings and their significance**

| Sr. No. | Tribe | Painting form | Description and meaning | Place in the house | Drawn by |
|---|---|---|---|---|---|
| 1. | Warli | *(a)* Dev chowk | Chowk means square with Dev (God) in it. This is drawn by married women (suhasinis) on the first day of the wedding. The Dev Chowk has in the centre mother earth (palghat), and other Gods such as the sun, Moon, Hirva, Haimi, Waghdev, Panch Shiryu, besides other figures of cultural significance. The chowk is drawn with rice paste and believed to have the Gods come on earth to bless the new couple to the fertile. | The wall of the living room facing the east, from the where the sun rises. | Married women (the Suhasinis) |
| | | *(b)* Lagna Chowk | Like the Dev Chowk, Lagna chowk is a square in which a horse on which the bride and groom are shown sitting, along with a band of musicians and marriage procession. | It is drawn on the wall | Married woman (suhasinis). |

*(Contd…)*

| Sr. No. | Tribe | Painting form | Description and meaning | Place in the house | Drawn by |
|---|---|---|---|---|---|
| | | *(c)* Kanna the symbol of viginity | Kanna is a rice powder painting drawn by married women on a pounding hole. It is a squarish painting with a multiplication sign meaning the virginity status of the bride. The painting in decorated with turmeric and kumkum and symbolises the vagina of the bride. | drawn on the pounding hole in the living room on the third day of the warli wedding. | Married women (Suhasinis) |
| | | *(d)* Murthi-symbol of prosperity | Murthi are fist marks of rice paste of worli women printed on the side of door post after the harvest | on the side of the door post | Mothers of every worli house. |
| | | *(e)* Bhavru | A rice powder is painting drawn on the third day of the worli wedding having five circular patterns. This symbolises fertility time after menstruation. | Drawn in the Kitchen, the living room the verandah and the courtyard five terms. | Married women (Suhasinis) |
| 2. | Rathwa of Gujarat | *(a)* Pithoro | Most respected God of the Rathwas. The God of household as well as cattle welfare. | wall in the living room | Married men |
| | | *(b)* Pithoro | wife of pithoro riding a house | wall in the living room | Married men |
| | | *(c)* Situ Rano | Foster father of Pithoro | wall in the living room | Married men |
| | | *(d)* Kali Koyal | Mother of Pithoro | wall in the living room | Married men |

*(Contd...)*

| Sr. No. | Tribe | Painting form | Description and meaning | Place in the house | Drawn by |
|---|---|---|---|---|---|
| | | (e) Rani Kajol | Foster mother of pithoro. Besides this several other figures, horses, animals and legendary heros and drawn with rock colours. | wall in the living room | married men |
| 3. | Saora | wall painting | Saora wall painting of ferlity, Gods and goddesses spirits, festivals, marriage, birth and death are depicted in the coloured paintings | wall in the living room | married men |
| 4. | Gonds of Madhya Pradesh | wall painting | Gond women paint the walls with rock colours as well as rice paste, in order to appear the Gods and goddesses of house welfare, prosperity and fertility. | wall in the living room as well as outer wall of the entrance | married women |
| 5. | Bhils of Madhya Pradesh | wall painting | Icons and images of wild animals, Gods and Goddesses, spirits cosmic beings/forces are drawn to appear them for protection welfare and fertility. | wall in the living room as well as the outer wall of the entrance | married women |

respectively. These paintings are a form of communication to communicate to the younger generation about religion, sexual life, married and family life, cosmos, taboos, and other aspects of cultural.

An informal dialogue with the painters, both women and men from Rathwa tribe of Gujarat; Bhils and Gonds of Madhya Pradesh; Saoras of Orissa and the Worlis of Maharashtra, it was observed that certain paintings are drawn by these groups on the wall, in the kitchen, on the pounding hole, in the courtyard etc. have cultural significance.

These paintings reflect the vitality of living, the patterns of memory, a cultural philosophy and traditional communication forms besides an extensive and geometric vocabulary depicting the world view of the tribe. In this case study an attempt has been made by the researcher to present the tribe, then painting forms, the place of painting in the house and the meanings they associated with it.

### (3) Analysis

A detailed analysis of the symbolism meanings the Warlis, Gonds, Bhils, Saoras and Rathwas associated with their respective painting cults in given in the book entitled, "Threads Together" by Dr. Tribhuwan Robin and Finkenauer Maike (2003). The paintings as well as the spots where they are drawn mean a lot to the tribals. These small details need to be kept in mind while planning housing projects.

## CASE STUDY NO. 13

### (1) Aim of the Case Study

To understand how important "lofts" are to the Kokna community.

### (2) Background

Bharsatmet village is located about 16 kms. away from Jawahar tahsil of Thane district, in the state of Maharashtra. The village is predominantly inhabited by the Kikna tribe. The total population of the village as per 1991 census is 1600.

Bharsatmet is popular for 'Bohada'—the mask festival. In their 'Bohada'—the mask festival. In their book captained, "Tribal Masks and Myths", Tribhuwan Robin and Savelli Laurence (2003) have provided a detailed account, analysis and interpretation of the Bohada festival. In this case study an attempt has been made to highlight how valuable and sacred are the masks and the 'lofts'—the places where they are kept.

### (3) The Mask Characters

Tribals of Jawahar, Mokhada and peth tahsils of Thane and Nasik districts have revealed that there are 52 different characters of masks made up of paper masche, wood, cowdung and clay, and bamboo are made and displayed in dramatic action during the Bohada festival. However, in Bharsatmet it was discovered that there are 30 traditional mask characters, owned by 30 clans. There 30 characters are:

1. Narandev
2. Masa or Fish
3. Sarjadevi or Saraswati-peacock
4. Ganesh or Ganpati
5. Mahadev
6. Indra dev
7. Khanderao
8. Kaloba
9. Niloba
10. Bhairoba
11. Kalbhairi
12. Ram tati
13. Kaurav tati
14. Hedumba
15. Mhaisasur
16. Bakasur

17. Ravan
18. Vishnu Dev
19. Chand Dev
20. Surya Dev
21. Bhim-Bakasur
22. Raktadevi
23. Ghubadevi
24. Agnidevi
25. Landhya
26. Narsihva
27. Satwai
28. Bibisan
29. Kumbha Karna (Ravan's brother)
30. Krishna

These masks are possessed by 30 clans in the village. Interestingly when Dr. Tribhuwan and Savelli conducted their research it was observed that every head of the clan keeps there masks in a basket with their faces covered with a piece of sari cloth. The masks are then kept on the loft in their respective houses. As a cultural norm they are removed only few days before, the Bchada festival if they require repairing and painting. In order to do that head of the house opens the sari cloth tied on the mask only after breaking a coconut.

## Analysis

Lofts, among the Koknas are sacred spots for keeping gods and masks in baskets, hence lofts gain cultural significance. Besides keeping gods in the booklets the Koknas keep their food grain baskets on the lofts seed baskets and other agricultural implements. The place of gods near the grain banks could be serving the function of protection, may be to keep robbers and thieves away.

## CASE STUDY NO. 14

1. **Aim of the Case Study:** To highlight the factors that influenced a Warli painter to build a toilet in the back yard of his house.

2. **Background:** Rajesh Chintya Wangad, aged, 32, a member of Warli tribe and a resident of 'Wangad pada' in Ganjad village. Rajesh has been a commercial Warli painter for almost 15 years. He goes to cities like New Delhi, Bombay, Pune, Udaipur, Bhopal etc., for selling his paintings in the exhibitions. He has learnt to handle urban customers and business very well. He printed his business card as well.

3. **Urban and Modern Influence:** The result of urban and modern influence on Rajesh's life was that he married an educated Warli girl. He started to dress up like modern people, opened a bank account, saved money and brought second hand sumo car which is used for transporting people. To sum up Rajesh has progressed socially and economically.

4. **What made him to build a toilet?:** Several trips to cities and towns for exhibitions, exposed Rajesh to urban about building a toilet and a bathroom for himself and his family members. He collected money and built a small toilet and a bathroom in the backyard of his house. He spend enough money to built the toilet and bathroom, after consulting a builder.

Rajesh also made efforts to learn toilet habits and style of maintaining the toilet and bathroom. He educated his family members. There is harpic cleaning sudation in his toilet and bathroom, including a scribing brush. The women folk of the house clean the toilet with harpic.

### (4) Analysis

Exposure of Rajesh to urban and modern influence, helped him to think rationally, consult right people, rationally, consult right people, educate himself his family about toilet habits. This case study must remind the policy makers and administrators, that it is necessary to educate people about any program to be implemented for them. Rajesh spend time to educate himself and his family members, gained knowledge about toilet habits and its maintenance and then built one.

## CASE STUDY NO. 15

1. **Aim of the case study:** To highlight the process of building an art centre for the Warli artisans of Raitali village.

2. **Background:** Raitali village is located in Dahanu tahsil of Thane district of Maharashtra state. The village is 13 kms. away from Dahanu its tahsil head quarters. Its famous for Warli artisans. The institute of Development Educational Activities and Studies (IDEAS), Pune has designed a plan with some artisans to build a small Warli art centre.

   A meeting of Warli artisans was called by the president of IDEAS. He explained to the artisans the need to build this centre. The centre also expressed their views abut the same. Nathu Dehu Sutar volunteered to donate his land for the project. Shanker Chipad, Chintu Rajad, Pandu Rajad said they will contribute labour for building the centre. Nathu's mother and his wife V volunteered to maintain the centre and provide security to the same.

   The official of IDEAS held another meeting with the village officials and put forth this proposal. The proposal was appreciated by the traditional as well as Government managed panchayat. Every co-operation from their side was assured.

3. **Analysis:** Proper discussion, right motivation and community organisation helps in making a project successful. When the building process will start IDEAS will involve the artisans as well as villagers in the project.

## CASE STUDY NO. 16

### (1) Aim of the Case Study

To explore the knowledge of tribals about Indira Awas Vikas Yojna the housing scheme.

### (2) Background

Shitful Worli is a tribal hamlet predominantly inhabited by the Katkari tribe. An attempt was made to understand how many Katkaris in this village are aware about the Indira Awas Vikas Yojna out of the 60 houses in the village all the house holds know about the scheme, but when details such as which department implements it? What documents have to be submitted? How much amount is sanctioned per house etc., the Katkaris did not know about the same. Almost all the villagers did not any thing regarding the scheme. They only know that the gram sevak (village level worker) takes a beneficiary to the bank and make him put a thumb impression on a paper and asks him to go home.

### (3) What is Indira Awas Yajana?

#### *(a) Introduction*

During the years 1985-86 the Indira Awas Yajana was part the Jawahar Rojgar Yojana. On January 1, 1996 till was declared as an independent scheme, in order to provide houses to the poor.

#### *(b) Objective of the Scheme*

The objective of the scheme was to help poor, landless members of scheduled tribes and scheduled castes from the rural areas to build and/or repair their houses, by giving them financial assistance.

#### *(c) Amount Sanctioned*

A sum of Rs. 28,500/- in sanction to match Rs. 1500/- from the beneficiary to build a house of Rs. 30,000.

#### *(d) Information about the scheme*

A booklet in Marathi has been printed by the Ministry of Rural Development, Government of Maharashtra and is available in Zilla Parishad at district head quarters, Panchayat Samiti at block level and Gram Sevak at village level.

### *(e) Who can be its beneficiary?*

*(i)* A member of scheduled tribe or caste.

*(ii)* A resident of rural area.

*(iii)* A person from B.P.L. family (Below the poverty line in earning less than Rs. 20,000 per year).

*(iv)* A person who has not been a beneficiary of this scheme earliest.

*(v)* A person whose house needs to be renovated.

### *(f) Identity of the beneficiary*

*(i)* Tribal identity certificate

*(ii)* B.P.L. card holder (yellow colour ration card)

*(iii)* Education identity care sometimes helps.

### *(g) Priority to select the beneficiary*

*(i)* Landless labourers

*(ii)* Poor members from the scheduled tribe or caste

*(iii)* Members from other backward, but economically weaker sections

*(iv)* Handicapped persons

*(v)* Ex-army man or a widow of a soldier.

*(vi)* Members from B.P.L. list.

### *(h) Handing Over*

It is compulsory to transfer the house either on woman's name or on both husband and wife's name.

### *(i) Land Selection Criteria*

The house should be build within the village land limits so that the owner of the house can avail facilities such as electricity, water, roads, ration shop etc.

### *(j) Who should Build?*

The program does not permit the public works department or a contractor to build the same. The beneficiary is asked to build the house himself.

### *(k) Area of the House*

The area of the house according to the scheme, should not be less than 20 sq. feet.

### *(l) Site Selection*

The building site of the house to be build or repaired should not be away from the village/hamlet.

### *(m) Smokeless Chulahs*

A chulah is an hearth or a fire place, used for cooking. According to the Indira Awas Yajana the owner of the new house should build a smokeless chulah in his house. This is to avoid, carbon monoxide from being inhaled by the households, especially children.

### *(n) Environment Development*

The beneficiary along with his fellow villagers is expected to plant trees in and around the village.

### *(o) Role of N.G.O's*

Government as well as the beneficiaries can work with genuine N.G.O's to plan the building of smokeless chulahs, reforestation, maintain cleanliness, build toilets etc.

### *(p) Declare the List of Beneficiaries*

The Gram Panchayat is expected to declare the names of beneficiaries of Indira Awas Yojana in the form of list which should be put upon the notice board of the Gram Panchayat. The Panchayat Samiti is suppose to check and monitor this.

### *(q) Monitoring*

Officials right from the state, district and block level should personally monitor the progress of the building or repair work and bring it to the notice of the central Government.

### *(r) Evaluation*

The officials of the State Government are expected to conduct an evaluation of the program from time to time.

### *(s) Budget Allocation*

The Central Government gives 80 per cent of the money to the state government, while 20 per cent of the share for this scheme has to be borne by the state government.

### *(t) Bank Account*

The amount sanctioned from this scheme must be kept separately in a bank or post office.

### *(u) Disbursement of Amount*

The beneficiary should be given money according to the progress of the construction.

### (4) Analysis

The researcher studied the Indira Awas Yojana, in detail and while cross checking it in the field, it was observed that over 98 per cent of the tribals are not aware about the details of the scheme. It is time to disseminate this information to the tribals, so that they are aware of their rights.

## CASE STUDY NO. 17

1. **Aim of the case study:** To study how non-tribal, rich farmers take advantage of the Indira Awas Yojana.
2. **Background:** Nehale is village, situated about 6-8 kms. away from Wada tahsil headquarters. It is close to the road. The village comprises of Warlis, Katkaris and the Maratha caste farmers.
3. **Course of Event:** Mr. X a member of the Warli tribe, aged 40, is a landless labourer working for a rich Maratha farmer Mr. Y in the same village. My Y helped Mr. X to get benefits of the Indira Awas Yajana, but on his own land under the name of the tribal. After the house was complete, Mr. Y asked Mr. X to go back to

his old house in the village. Mr. Y said the land on which Indira Awas Yajana house in built belongs to me. I have paid extra money to make good quality doors and windows including the roof, hence the house belongs to me. Mr. X who was poor, landless, illiterate and ignorant had to leave, as his sustenance and survival dependent on the employer.

4. **Analysis:** Many of such incidences take place, where in non-tribals who are socially and economically well off and politically influential take advantage of schemes by making the poor tribals scape goats. As Mr. Y did, he is currently using the house as a store room far keeping agricultural implement, fertilisers etc., in this house, while on paper Mr. X is the real beneficiary. Strict action must be taken against such corruption.

## CASE STUDY NO. 18

1. **Aim of the Case Study:** To understand or an average how much money is spent on the Indira Awas Yojana in a district, by the zilla parishad.

2. **Background:** Pune district comprises of 13 blocks or tahsils. The researcher made an attempt to explore how many houses were built and repaired and the amount spent on these during the financial year, 2002-2003.

An official from the Zilla Parishada, Pune was interviewed to find out the same.

3. **Findings:** It was observed that during the financial year 2002-2003 the Zilla Parishad, Pune completed construction and repair works of 2441 houses and spent 910.455 lakhs of rupees on Indira Awas Vikas Yojana, when enquired what must be the budget for the State, the official said it runs into crores. Table given below presents block wise houses completed and money spent on them during the year 2002-2003, in Pune district.

**Table No. 4.2: Blockwise number houses complete and project amount spent on Indira Awas Yojna during the year 2002-2003 in Pune district**

| Sl. No. | Block | No. of houses completed | Grant amount received | Grant spent (figures in lakhs) | |
|---|---|---|---|---|---|
| 1. | Ambegaon | 24 | 152 | 57.44 | 57.44 |
| 2. | Basamati | 152 | 365 | 137.51 | 137.51 |
| 3. | Bhor | 365 | 43 | 25.65 | 25.65 |
| 4. | Daund | 43 | 307 | 101.18 | 101.18 |
| 5. | Haveli | 307 | 153 | 57.66 | 57.66 |
| 6. | Indapur | 153 | 395 | 143.43 | 143.43 |
| 7. | Junnar | 395 | 306 | 126.13 | 126.13 |
| 8. | Khed | 306 | 223 | 84.74 | 84.74 |
| 9. | Maval | 223 | 122 | 44.74 | 44.74 |
| 10. | Mulshi | 55 | 55 | 21.22 | 21.22 |
| 11. | Purander | 87 | 87 | 33.01 | 33.01 |
| 12. | Shirur | 207 | 207 | 68.14 | 68.14 |
| 13. | Velha | 26 | 26 | 9.78 | 9.78 |
| | Total | 2441 | 2441 | 910.45 | 910.45 |

4. **Analysis:** From the above table it can be concluded that blocks such as Baramati and Indapur received maximum share of houses as well as money, though they are not tribal blocks, however the members of scheduled castes and other economically weaker sections could have received benefits. Thus, on an average an amount of Rs. 910.45 lakhs is spent an Pune district for implementing the Indira Awas Yojana, covering 2441 houses.

It is suggested that less housing targets of genuine beneficiaries could be covered by sanctioning at least Rs. 50,000/- per house, instead of Rs. 28,500/-. This will contribute in maintaining the quality of construction and use of good building material.

## CASE STUDY NO. 19

1. **Aim of the Case Study:** To calculate an average amount of wood used by a Kokna farmer to build his house.

2. **Background:** Koknas and Mahadev kolis are one of the progressive tribes in Maharashtra. Socially, economically, educationally and politically they are better off than the other groups. One of the characteristics of Koknas is the big houses made up of brick walls (recently) or stick walls, with tiled roofs. On an average a Kokna occupies at least 2000 to 3000 sq. feet area to build his house.

3. **Cost of the Forest Resources:** Koknas use teak, Khair tamarind and Jumun wood to build the pillars, beams, columns and roof of the house. Teak beams are also used in the cattle shed, which is usually at the backyard within the house.

Few residents of Bharsatmet village, in Jawahar Tahsil of Thane district were interviewed to find out the amount of wood cut for building their house. It was observed that on an average a Kokna who has over 10 acres of agricultural land uses eight teak wooden pillars of 8 inches, breadth and 12 to 14 feet height eight pillars as the main pillars which are inserted in the grandland. In between there pillars he makes a wall of Kanvi sticks which he gets from the forest. Another six pillars for building the cow shed at the back within the main house. Four same size pillars for supporting the roof. About 100 to 150 small wooden pillars to support the tiles. In the manager there is an horizontal pillar, 12 to 14 feet long, which rests on two pillars about 3 to 4 feet high. This is used for tying the cattle.

Building the loft requires 50 to 100 wooden planks. On the loft Koknas keep their food grains.

It was difficult to get the exact number of wooden pillars, planks and bamboos required to build a Kokna house on 2000 sq. feet land, but on an average a forest official told me that teak, Khair and Ain timber is very costly. If an estimate of the cost of a traditional Kokna house has to estimated it would run in lakhs of rupees.

The forest official also maintained that if one has to calculate the amount of wood used by tribals far building traditional houses it would be billions of tones. Besides urban demand for timber from the forest, the tribals themselves bank heavily on forest timber especially to build their houses, youth dermiteries, Samay Mandirs, houses of social significance etc.

4. **Analysis:** As compared to the cost of traditional tribal house which requires teak, ain, Khair and tamarind tree timber which is very expensive and also promotes loss of forest wealth, the Indira Awas Yojana houses are economical reasonable. Thus, some modifications need to be done in the scheme such as quality of material, material to be replaced, amount to be increased etc. The economics of the scheme, implementation procedure, the process of planning and monitoring needs to be worked out the strengthen the program, so as to meet the desired goal of the housing project.

## CASE STUDY NO. 20

1. **Aim of the Case Study:** To highlight the need of a documentation-cum-research all at the Panchayat Samiti level.
2. **Background:** During the year 2002-2003 a visit was made by the researcher to Panchayat Samitis in Maharashtra to find out statistics on housing program for last five years.
3. **Observation:** The names of the Panchayat Samities visited are not declared in this case study. It was surprising to note that:

   *(a)* It would take 2 to 4 hours to get information on one years out put and no information or incomplete information on last five years records.

   *(b)* No record room for maintaining records of housing scheme

   *(c)* Discrepancy in figures of beneficiaries covered under the Indira Awas Scheme for five years.

(*d*) No records of list of beneficiaries who received benefits.

(*e*) No documentation cell to give right kind of information.

(*f*) No proper public relation officer to give details of the scheme.

4. **Analysis:** An educated person like me has to face so many problems and hurdles, what about the poor, ignorant, illiterate, unempowered tribals. It is suggested that there is a need for setting up a documentation and guidance centre at the Panchayat Samiti and I.T.D.P. level to guide people about the schemes.

*****

# Chapter—5

# SUMMARY, CONCLUSIONS AND RECOMMENDATIONS

## 5.1 Summary

The Indira Awas Yojana is a major housing program implemented by the respective State Governments in the country. Eighty per cent of the grant for his eighty per cent for this program is given by the government of India, while twenty per cent is matched by the respective state government. The objectives of the scheme is to financially assist members of scheduled tribes and castes along with other socially and economically backward groups to build new houses and/or repair the old ones.

At the tahsil level, this scheme is implemented and monitored by the Panchayat Samiti. Gram Sevaks are the main personnel who actually see the project through at the village or hamlet level. Millions of rupees are spent on the scheme.

This book throws light on tribal peoples reactions to the scheme. It also presents recommendations to strengthen and modify the scheme so that it fits into tribal people's eco-cultural frame work. Besides this, the book also unveils the symbolism associated with house construction both from an insider's (tribal) as well as outsider's (etic) perspective. Findings reported in the book will help the policy makers and administrators to look into tribal housing projects positively, so as to give justice to the tribals and other weaker sections of Indian society.

## 5.2 Conclusions

Based on the primary data collected through informal in-depth interviews, case studies and observation following conclusions were drawn.

1. **Cultural Dimension:** Like the Hindus who believe in "Vastu Shashtra", tribals too have cultural interpretation of how their houses should be built. Failure on the part of administrators to understand the symbolism rituals, customs and traditions of house construction in tribal society (from an insiders (tribal) perspective has created a communication gap between tribal beneficiaries and the Gram Sevak".

2. **Awareness Regarding Indira Awas Yojana:** There is a wide gap in the understanding or knowledge of the beneficiary and the implementing machinery about the scheme. Tribals just know that there is a housing scheme, but they do not know which agency implements it? What are its objectives? For which section of Indian society the scheme is meant for? How much money is given to a beneficiary, etc.?

3. **The Toilet Scheme:** The toilet scheme for tribals in Nandurbar district is a:

    *(i)* lack of proper planning with tribals.

    *(ii)* lack of prior survey or research before planning and implementing the scheme.

    *(iii)* lack of dialogue with tribals to find out whether or not they need toilets.

    *(iv)* less or no water supply or tanks near/in the toilet.

    *(v)* no education or training package before launching the scheme.

    *(vi)* Positioning the toilets right in front of the house.

The scheme, though is not part of the Indira housing scheme, is very much associated with housing program if we view it broadly, hence the scheme was evaluated by the researcher. Hence it would be right to conclude that toilets should be provided only to those educated tribals who know how to *use* and *maintain* it. These are cases of tribals who use toilets, but are very few.

4. **Quality of Construction:** *(a)* Quality of Indira housing scheme depends a lot on the interest taken by the grass root level officials in monitoring and checking whether or not good cement, bricks and other items needed for construction are bought, *(b)* Secondly, the exact amount of Rs. 28,500/- spent on the scheme. *(c)* Thirdly, personal interest and extra financial contribution of the beneficiary also helps in attaining quality of construction.

5. **Economics of Traditional Houses:** "The cost of traditional houses of "economically better of tribals works out to be more because of use of teak wood "in large quantities, as compared to the Indira Awas Yojana".

6. **Research, Documentation and Maintaining Cell:** Establishment research-cum-documentation cell at the Panchayat Samiti level could contribute to maintain proper record, Statistics and other details of the scheme implemented by the Panchayat Samiti, including housing scheme.

## 5.3 Recommendations

Given the background of case studies and tribal people's perceptions reported in the book, following recommendations will help the policy, makes, administrators of government departments as well as other agencies implementing housing projects, for tribals.

*(i)* Efforts should be made to understand the cultural rationale and symbolism as viewed by a tribal community in constructing the house. Their customs, rituals, traditions should be respected and incorporated while constructing the house.

*(ii)* **Involving Tribal Key Personnel:** Involving traditional tribal carpenters, builders, workers and other

functionaries in building the house will be a bonus for the beneficiary. There key persons may be taken financial incentives.

*(iii)* **Awareness about the Scheme:** It is necessary on in depth understanding of Indira Awas Yojana given to the beneficiary. This will help him to the psychologically ready and plan his budget as well. If he is told one year in advance that he will be a beneficiary of the scheme next year, the tribal can save extra money, instead of Rs. 1500/-.

*(iv)* **Need for a Research, Documentation-cum Maintaining Unit:** There is an urgent need to establish a research, documentation and monitoring unit at the panchayat samiti level of evaluate the impact of the schemes, maintain proper statistics, records as well as monitor the on going schemes, including housing schemes.

*(v)* **Increase Budget:** Currently the construction cost of building a new house, under Indira Awas Yojana in Rs. 28,500/- with the contribution of 1500/- from the beneficiary, should be increased to Rs. 50,000/- so as to maintain quality of the house.

*(vi)* **Quality Control:** Strict watch on the quality of material used for the house should be kept.

*(vii)* **Physical Audit:** Physical verification of the housing project gives a clearer and true picture, than auditing bills and vouchers.

*(viii)* **Settlement Planning:** Housing program should not restrict to building a house or two for B.P.L. tribals in a village.

Infact it would be ideal to have long term planning of the settlement. This would include construction of:

*(a)* I.C.D.S. (Anganwadi) unit

*(b)* Clinic

(c) Samaj Mandir

(d) Grain Bank

(e) Veterinary service unit

(f) Ration shop

(g) Primary school

(h) Water tank for the cattle

(i) Wells/Bore wells/Hand pumps

(j) Flour mill

(k) Shop

(l) Electricity

(m) Roads

(n) Adult education centre

(o) Chavdi

(p) Tree plantation etc.

As rightly said by a Bhil beneficiary from Nimbori village of Nandurbar district, that I will feel that my "pada" (hamlet) has developed if the above facilities are available in my hamlet.

(ix) **Tiles for Tin Sheets:** Tribals prefer tiles instead of tin and cement sheets for their roofs. Tiled roof gives a cooling effect, where tin sheets make the environment in the house hot.

*****

# REFERENCES


1. Aglaja Stirn and Peter Van Ham, 2003, *The Hidden World of the Naga* (Living Traditions in Northeast India and Burma), Prestel, Munich.
2. Tribhuwan Robin, 1998, *Medical world of Tribals*, Discovery Publishing House, New Delhi.
3. Tribhuwan Robin and Finkenauer Maike, 2003, *Threads Together*, Discovery Publishing House, New Delhi.
4. Tribhuwan Robin and Savelli, L., 2003, *Tribal Masks and Myth*, Discovery Publishing House, Discovery publishing House, New Delhi.
5. Tribhuwan Robin (ed), 2000, *Studies in Tribal, Rural and Urban Development*, Discovery publishing House, New Delhi.
6. Jain N.S. and Tribhuwan Robin, 1996, *Mirage of Health and Development*, Vidyanidhi Publications, Pune.
7. Jain N.S., and Tribhuwan Robin (ed) 1995, *An Overview of Tribal Research Studies*, TR and TI, Pune.
8. Booklet on Indira Awas Yojana, 1998, Ministry of Rural Development, Government of India, Delhi.


❋❋❋❋❋